❊ *Making beautiful* ❊

christmas cakes

D1306918

❄ *Making beautiful* ❄

christmas cakes

MEREHURST

Contents

Equipment & Ingredients

Airbrush for spraying food colouring.

Ball tool available in various sizes and used to make depressions, such as eye sockets, or to cup small pieces of paste to form ears, leaves, etc.

Cake boards available as single and double thickness card, thin hardboard and 1cm (½in) thickness drums.

Cake scrapers to smooth royal icing on the sides of a cake.

Cake stands shapes and sizes are available to suit all cakes.

Cake tins (pans) it is useful to have a variety of sizes and shapes.

Clear alcohol for thinning colours and sticking sugarpaste to a marzipan covering.

Clingfilm (plastic wrap) for wrapping paste while it is not in use to prevent it from drying out.

Cocktail sticks (toothpicks) used for modelling and texturing, and for adding colouring to icing. They can also be rolled across the edge of a Garrett frill to splay out the scalloped edges.

Cornflour (cornstarch) to dust surfaces when modelling items.

Crimpers for making patterns in sugarpaste and marzipan.

Cutters available in many shapes, avoiding the need for templates.

Dresden tool has a sharp, or veining, end used for scoring paste, making small pinpricks and rolling paste, and a blunt end for scoring and making oval depressions and grooves. It is also useful for frilling and fluting.

Dusting powders (petal dusts) for brushing colour onto the surface of pastes.

Edible glue made from water and powdered gum, used to stick sugar pieces together.

Edible varnish for adding a sheen to decorative pieces.

Embossing tools for decorating sugarpaste and marzipan.

Fine mesh sieve useful for sifting icing sugar before use.

Firm foam sponge for thinning and shaping flowerpaste pieces.

Florist's wire available in various thicknesses, or gauges, and used to support model work.

Flowerpaste (gum paste) used primarily for creating hand-modelled flowers and other delicate decorations that require a hard-setting paste.

Foam sponge for supporting decorative pieces while drying.

Food colourings available as paste, liquid, jelly and powder.

Garrett frill a sugarpaste frill with a scalloped edge.

Greaseproof (parchment) paper for baking and templates.

Grooved non-stick board for rolling out paste to make flower petals and leaves where wiring is required.

Glycerine added to royal icing for easy cutting.

Gum arabic a firming agent exuded from acacia.

Gum tragacanth a firming agent to make paste set hard very quickly.

Icing (confectioners') sugar for royal icing and dusting work surfaces when rolling out marzipan and other pastes.

Liquid glucose adds elasticity to royal icing.

Marzipan (almond icing) almond-flavoured cake covering used as a base for royal icing and sugarpaste to produce a smooth surface. Can also be used to model decorative shapes.

Modelling tools available in many shapes for a variety of tasks.

Moulds for shaping decorations.

Painting solution mixes with dusting powder for painting.

Palette knife for spreading royal icing; use a crank-handled palette knife for lifting run-out work.

Pastillage a stiff, white paste used for making flowers and models. When dry, it resembles fine china.

Plaque a piece of sugarpaste, pastillage or flowerpaste that is attached to a cake for decoration. It can be embellished in numerous ways.

Plunger cutters cut out a shape and impress a design.

Rolling pins it is useful to have large and small sizes; white polypropylene pins are recommended.

Royal icing used to cover cakes, this is traditionally white but can also be coloured. It can be formed into peaks or piped, or thinned and 'flooded' into pre-drawn shapes.

Run-out film for creating run-out and piped-off pieces.

Sharp knife essential for making clean, accurate and straight cuts.

Smoothers to smooth and shape marzipan and sugarpaste.

Spare cake boards for decorating cakes on before transferring to the decorated board.

Straight edge for smoothing the top of royal-iced cakes.

Sugarpaste (rolled fondant) a soft, pliable paste that is rolled out and used to form a smooth coating on a cake.

Textured rolling pins for decorating sugarpaste surfaces.

Tilting turntables make working on the sides of a cake much easier.

Veiners for impressing veins on petals and leaves.

Whisk to beat ingredients manually.

White tile for mixing colours.

Basic cake recipes

Most fruit cakes will keep for 8 to 12 months, tightly wrapped with clingfilm (plastic wrap) and stored in an airtight container. Cakes containing nuts only keep for up to 3 months. Fruit cakes can be frozen.

Fruit cake

500g (1lb/3cups) sultanas
(golden raisins)
375g (12oz/2½cups) raisins, chopped
250g (8oz/1½cups) currants
250g (8oz/2cups) chopped glacé cherries
250ml (8floz/1cup) brandy or rum
250g (8oz/1cup) butter
230g (7½oz/1cup) soft, dark brown sugar
2tbsp apricot jam (jelly)
2tbsp treacle or syrup
1tbsp grated lemon or orange rind
4 eggs
350g (11oz/2¾cups) plain
(all-purpose) flour
1tsp ginger
1tsp mixed spice
1tsp cinnamon

1 Put the fruit in a bowl with the brandy and soak overnight. Preheat the oven to 150°C/ 300°F/ gas mark 2. Line a 23cm (9in) round cake tin (pan) (see pages 16–17).

2 Beat the butter and sugar. Beat in the jam (jelly), treacle and rind. Add the eggs, beating after each addition. Stir in the fruit and the sifted flour and spices.

3 Spoon into the tin and smooth the surface. Tap the tin to remove air bubbles. Place on layers of newspaper in the oven and bake for 3 to 3½ hours, or until a skewer comes out clean. Brush with brandy. Cover with greaseproof (parchment) paper and wrap in a tea (kitchen) towel. Leave to cool in the tin.

Light fruit cake

185g (6oz/¾cup) unsalted butter
125g (4oz/½cup) caster
(superfine) sugar
3 eggs
160g (5½oz/1cup) sultanas
(golden raisins)
100g (3½oz/⅔cup) currants
60g (2oz/¼cup) chopped glacé apricots
45g (1½oz/¼cup) chopped glacé figs
250g (8oz/2cups) chopped glacé cherries
80g (2¾oz/½cup) coarsely chopped macadamia nuts
185g (6oz/1½cups) plain
(all-purpose) flour
60g (2oz/½cup) self-raising flour
125ml (4floz/½cup) milk
1tbsp sweet sherry
Nuts or glacé cherries

1 Preheat the oven to 160°C/ 315°F/ gas mark 2–3. Line a deep 20cm (8in) round cake tin (pan) (see pages 16–17). Cream the softened butter and sugar in a bowl until just combined. Add the eggs, beating well after each addition.

2 Transfer to a large bowl and stir in the fruit and nuts. Sift in half the flours and milk and stir. Stir in the remaining flours, milk and the sherry. Spoon into the tin and tap to remove air bubbles.

Smooth the surface with wet fingers and decorate with nuts or cherries. Wrap the outside of the tin (see pages 16–17). Place on layers of newspaper in the oven and bake for 1¾ to 2 hours or until a skewer comes out clean.

3 Remove from the oven, and wrap in a tea (kitchen) towel until cool. Remove the tin lining and wrap the cake in foil, or store in an airtight container.

Low-cholesterol cake

1kg (2lb/4cups) mixed dried fruit
160g (5½oz/⅔cup) chopped glacé apricots
140g (4½oz/⅔cup) chopped glacé pineapple
250ml (8floz/1cup) brandy
230g (7½oz/1cup) soft brown sugar
80ml (2¼floz/⅓cup) vegetable oil
3 egg whites, lightly beaten
1tsp vanilla essence (extract)
1tbsp molasses
1tbsp orange marmalade
2tbsp orange rind, finely grated
250g (8oz/2cups) plain (all-purpose) flour
60g (2oz/½cup) self-raising flour
1tsp ground nutmeg
1tsp ground cinnamon
1tsp ground cloves
1tsp mixed spice

1 Mix the fruit in a large bowl with the brandy. Cover and leave overnight. Preheat the oven to 150ºC/ 300ºF/ gas mark 2. Line a deep 23cm (9in) round cake tin (pan) (see pages 16–17).

2 Beat the sugar, oil and egg whites. Add the essence, molasses, marmalade and rind and beat. Transfer to a large bowl and stir in the fruit and sifted dry ingredients. Spoon into the tin, tap to remove any air bubbles and smooth the surface with wet fingers. Wrap the outside of the tin (see pages 16–17). Place on layers of newspaper in the oven and bake for 3 hours, or until a skewer inserted into the cake comes out clean.

3 Remove from the oven and cover with greaseproof (parchment) paper then foil. Wrap in a tea (kitchen) towel until cool.

Sugar-reduced cake

1.25kg (2½lb/5cups) mixed dried fruit
250ml (8floz/1cup) brandy
185g (6oz/¾cup) unsalted butter
125g (4oz/½cup) soft brown sugar
4 eggs, lightly beaten
2tbsp coffee and chicory essence
1tbsp finely grated orange rind
250g (8oz/2cups) plain (all-purpose) flour
60g (2oz/½cup) self-raising flour
1tsp ground nutmeg
1tsp ground cinnamon
1tsp mixed spice
¼tsp ground cloves
125g (4oz/1¼cups) pecans

1 Mix the fruit in a large bowl with the brandy. Cover and leave overnight, stirring occasionally. Grease and line a deep 23cm (9in) round cake tin (pan) (see pages 16–17). Preheat the oven to 150ºC/ 300ºF/ gas mark 2.

2 Beat the softened butter and sugar. Add the eggs, beating well after each addition. Add the essence and rind and beat until combined. Transfer to a large bowl and stir in the fruit and sifted dry ingredients. Spoon into the cake tin, tap the tin to remove any air bubbles and smooth the surface with wet fingertips. Decorate with the pecans. Wrap the outside of the tin (see pages 16–17).

3 Place the cake on layers of newspaper in the oven and bake for 2¾ to 3 hours, or until a skewer comes out clean. Cover with greaseproof (parchment) paper then foil. Wrap in a tea (kitchen) towel and leave to cool in the tin.

Chocolate mud cake

250g (8oz/1cup) butter
250g (8oz) dark chocolate
2tbsp instant espresso coffee powder
or granules
150g (5oz/1¼cups) self-raising flour
150g (5oz/1¼cups) plain
(all-purpose) flour
60g (2oz/½cup) cocoa powder
½tsp bicarbonate of soda
550g (1lb 2oz/2¼cups) caster
(superfine) sugar
4 eggs
2tbsp oil
125ml (4floz/½cup) buttermilk

1 Preheat the oven to 160ºC/ 315ºF/
gas mark 2–3. Grease and line a deep
23cm (9in) round cake tin (pan)
(see pages 16–17).

2 Put the butter, chocolate and coffee
in a pan with 185ml (6floz) hot water.
Stir over low heat until smooth.

3 Sift the flours, cocoa and bicarbonate
of soda into a large bowl. Stir in the
sugar and make a well in the centre.
Add the combined eggs, oil and
buttermilk and, using a large metal
spoon, slowly stir to start incorporating
the dry ingredients. Gradually stir in
the melted chocolate mixture.

4 Pour into the tin and bake for
1¾ hours, or until a skewer comes out
clean. The skewer may appear slightly
wet. Remove from the oven unless the
centre looks uncooked. If it does, give
it an extra 5 to 10 minutes.

5 Leave the cake in the tin until it is
completely cold, then turn out and
wrap in clingfilm (plastic wrap).

Genoese cake

300g (10oz/2½cups) plain
(all-purpose) flour
8 eggs
225g (7oz/¾cup) caster (superfine) sugar
100g (3½oz/⅓cup) butter, melted

1 Preheat the oven to 180ºC/ 350ºF/
gas mark 4. Grease and line a deep,
23cm (9in) round cake tin (pan)
(see pages 16–17). Dust the tins lightly
with a little extra flour, shaking off the
excess. Sift the flour three times onto
greaseproof (parchment) paper.

2 Mix the eggs and sugar in a large
heatproof bowl. Place the bowl over a
pan of simmering water and beat with
electric beaters for 8 minutes, or until
the mixture is thick and fluffy. Remove
from the heat and beat for a further
3 minutes, or until slightly cooled.

3 Add the cooled butter and sifted
flour. Using a large metal spoon, fold
in quickly and lightly until the mixture
is just combined.

4 Spread the mixture evenly into the tin.
Bake for 35 to 40 minutes, or until the
sponge is slightly golden and shrinks
lightly from the side of the tin.

5 Leave the cake in the tin for 5 minutes
before turning out onto a wire rack
to cool.

Gingerbread

410g (13oz/3¼cups) self-raising flour
2tsp ground ginger
½tsp ground cloves
125g (4oz/½cup) firm unsalted butter
125g (4oz/⅔cup) dark muscovado sugar
125g (4oz/⅓cup) black treacle
(molasses)
1 egg, lightly beaten

1 Preheat the oven to 200°C/ 400°F/
gas mark 6. Grease and line two baking
(cookie) sheets (see pages 16–17).

2 Put the flour and spices in a
food processor. Cut the butter into
small pieces, add to the processor
and blend until the mixture
resembles breadcrumbs.

3 Add the sugar, treacle (molasses)
and egg to the processor and mix to
a dough. Remove from the processor,
wrap and chill in the refrigerator for
at least 30 minutes.

4 Roll out the dough on a floured
surface. Cut out the required shapes and
place them on the baking sheets. Bake
for 12 to 15 minutes until the shapes
have risen slightly and appear a little
paler in colour. Leave for 2 minutes,
then transfer to a wire rack to cool.

Variation: This recipe produces a rich,
dark gingerbread, ideal for making the
gingerbread house on page 90. However,
if you prefer lighter gingerbread, use
light muscovado sugar instead of dark
and golden (corn) syrup instead of black
treacle (molasses).

Butter cake

280g (9oz/1¼cups) butter
225g (7oz/¾cup) caster
(superfine) sugar
1½tsp vanilla essence (extract)
4 eggs
225g (7oz/1¾cups) self-raising flour
150g (5oz/1¼cups) plain
(all-purpose) flour
185ml (6floz/¾cup) milk

1 Preheat the oven to 180°C/ 350°F/
gas mark 4. Grease and line a deep
20cm (8in) round cake tin (pan)
(see pages 16–17).

2 Beat the butter and sugar until light
and creamy. Beat in the essence. Add the
eggs, beating well after each addition.

3 Fold in the combined sifted flours
alternately with the milk, until you get a
smooth mixture. Spoon into the tin and
smooth the surface. Bake for 1¼ hours,
or until a skewer comes out clean.

4 Leave in the tin for at least 5 minutes
then turn out onto a wire rack to cool.

Coconut cake

250g (8oz/2cups) self-raising flour
45g (1½oz/½cup) desiccated coconut
225g (7oz/¾cup) caster
(superfine) sugar
60g (2oz/½cup) ground almonds
250ml (8floz/1cup) buttermilk
2 eggs
1tsp vanilla essence (extract)
150g (5oz/⅔cup) butter, melted

1 Preheat the oven to 180°C/ 350°F/
gas mark 4. Grease and line a deep
20cm (8in) round cake tin (pan)
(see pages 16–17).

2 Mix the sifted flour, coconut, sugar
and almonds. Make a well in the centre.

3 Pour the combined buttermilk,
eggs, vanilla and butter into the well
and stir until smooth. Pour into the tin
and smooth the surface. Bake for 1 hour,
or until a skewer comes out clean when
inserted into the centre of the cake.

4 Leave in the tin for 10 minutes then
turn out onto a wire rack to cool.

Basic decorating techniques

A truly beautiful iced cake starts with careful preparation when making the cake. The more perfectly shaped the cake the better the result. So, organize yourself well, be patient and a beautiful cake will be your reward.

You will need 1kg (2lb) of marzipan (almond icing) and 1kg (2lb) of sugarpaste (rolled fondant) for a 23cm (9in) cake. Both are available in packets at supermarkets or cake-decorating shops. Keep them covered with clingfilm (plastic wrap) until needed in order to prevent them from drying out.

Marzipan (almond icing)

Most royal-iced cakes require a crisp, right-angled edge between the top and the sides. This can be created with a marzipan covering. When rolling out marzipan, use icing (confectioners') sugar so the marzipan does not stick. Knead the marzipan to make it pliable.

Fill any holes on the surface of the cake with small pieces of marzipan. Warm 2 tablespoons of apricot jam (jelly) with 1 teaspoon of water in a small pan over low heat, then push it through a fine sieve and brush it over the cake with a pastry brush. This acts as a 'glue'.

Roll out the marzipan into a circle large enough to cover the base and side of the cake. To prevent tearing the icing as you lift it, roll it over a rolling pin, then unroll and smooth it over the base and side of the cake. Dust your hands with icing sugar and press out any folds and wrinkles. Carefully pierce air bubbles with a large pin. Trim around the base of the cake with a sharp knife and leave to dry overnight in a cool, dry place. Ideally, leave for 1 to 2 days to make sure the cake has a really firm covering.

Sugarpaste (rolled fondant)

You can make sugarpaste or buy it. Commercially produced paste is high quality, available in a wide range of colours and usually more reliable.

Making sugarpaste

This recipe produces a good general purpose paste and is simple to make.

1 egg white
2tbsp liquid glucose
500g (1lb/4cups) icing (confectioners') sugar, sifted

1 Put the egg white and glucose into a bowl. Beat in the icing (confectioners') sugar until the mixture becomes stiff.

2 Knead the paste on a surface dusted with icing sugar until soft and pliable.

Covering a cake with sugarpaste

Roll out the paste and cover the cake using the same method as for marzipan (see page 12). Brush the surface of the marzipan with clear alcohol, then lift the sugarpaste onto the cake. Stroke the top of the cake with a smoother in the same direction as you are laying down the paste to expel any air. Allow the paste to fall down the side of the cake, open up any folds and ease back onto the side of the cake for a smooth surface. If the cake is square, cup your hand around the corner and stroke the paste upwards to prevent cracking on the corners.

Dust your hands with icing sugar or use a smoother to smooth out wrinkles and folds. Trim the paste around the base of the cake with a sharp knife and leave to dry overnight in a cool, dry place.

Colouring sugarpaste

Paste food colourings are most suitable for sugarpaste, but if delicate colours are required, it is possible to use liquid. Add the liquid colour one drop at a time, using a cocktail stick (toothpick).

When left, the colours mature and usually deepen. Sometimes, even though the paste has been well kneaded, spots of colour appear in the paste, spoiling the appearance. For this reason, you should leave the paste for a few hours, or overnight. Knead again before use.

Storing sugarpaste

Wrap leftover paste in clingfilm (plastic wrap), place in a polythene bag and store in an airtight container. Home-made paste keeps for up to 1 week, bought paste for 1 to 2 months.

Royal icing

Royal icing is extremely versatile – it can be spread to give a flawlessly smooth top coating to fruit cakes, piped into bulbs, loops and scrolls, or thinned down into run-icing.

Making royal icing with a mixer

Using an electric mixer is quicker and enables you to make large quantities.

45g (1½oz) albumen powder
300ml (10floz/1¼cups) water
1.75kg (3½lb/14cups) icing (confectioners') sugar, sifted

1 Dissolve the albumen powder in the water, strain and measure out 300ml (10floz/1¼cups).

2 Place the liquid in a clean mixer bowl together with the icing (confectioners') sugar, and stir.

3 Using an electric mixer, set to the slowest speed, beat the mixture until the required consistency is reached.

Making royal icing by hand

Do not attempt to make more than 500g (1lb) at one time.

30g (1oz) albumen powder
4tbsp water
500g (1lb/4cups) icing (confectioners') sugar, sifted

1 Dissolve the albumen in the water, then strain. Place in a large, clean bowl.

2 Add the icing (confectioners') sugar one tablespoon at a time, and beat. It will take about 20 minutes for the icing to reach soft peak consistency.

Covering a cake with royal icing

Three coats of royal icing should be applied to a marzipanned (almond-iced) cake (see page 12). Leave the icing to dry for 8 hours between layers. Use soft-peak icing for the first coat, then add water to soften slightly for the second. Soften again for the final coat.

Top coating
Spread a little royal icing over the top of the cake (round or square) with a palette knife. Hold the knife horizontally and work it backwards and forwards, while turning the cake, to eliminate any air bubbles. Spread evenly to the edges of the cake. Remove the cake from the turntable and place it onto a clean work surface. Draw a clean straight edge or long-bladed knife over the top of the cake in one continuous movement in order to create a smooth finish. Leave the icing to dry before coating the side of the cake.

Side coating a round cake
Place the cake on a turntable and start applying the royal icing to the side with a palette knife. Hold the knife vertically and position your finger down the back of the blade to apply pressure to the icing and disperse air bubbles. Rotate the cake and paddle the icing as you work to form an even thickness.

Make sure that the icing covers the cake from top to bottom and that no marzipan can be seen. Trim the excess from the top edge. Pull a plain cake scraper around the cake in one even movement, while rotating the turntable. When the scraper has been pulled around the whole cake, pull it off towards yourself to finish. This will leave a 'take-off' mark which will be removed later.

Side coating a square cake
Coat the first side of a square cake in the same way as a round cake. Move the scraper along the side and, at the end of the side, pull it off towards yourself. Start the second side by bringing the 'take-off' mark from the previous side around and onto the second side.

Repeat this process until all four sides of the cake are coated. Always ensure that all the edges are neat before leaving to dry and applying a second or third coat. Smooth any rough edges or surfaces with a sharp knife or scalpel.

Coating a board with royal icing

Coating cake boards can be done in two ways. The easier method is to leave the board until you have finished coating the final side of the cake. Then, while the icing is still wet, coat the board with a soft consistency of icing, resembling thick run-icing. Smooth the top with a palette knife, without removing any of the icing. Trim any excess icing from the edge of the board, then allow it to dry.

Alternatively, for a better finish, coat the board separately from the cake. Smaller sizes of boards can be coated with icing all the way across. Larger boards should be coated with an 8cm (3in) band of icing around the edge.

Remove the cake from the temporary cake board by scoring around the base with a scalpel before gently lifting it off.

Colouring royal icing

Many food colourings are suitable for use with royal icing. The most suitable, however, is liquid colouring, which mixes in easily. The main advantage is that it can be measured into the icing with a dropper. Count the number of drops of liquid colouring added to each 500g (1lb) royal icing to achieve the desired shade. This way, a colour can be repeated accurately for other batches of icing, if required later. Paste food colourings are not recommended for use with royal icing, except for very small quantities when an accurate match of the colour is not required.

Storing royal icing

Store in an airtight container, wrapped with clingfilm (plastic wrap) – no need to refrigerate. Re-beat to its original consistency at least every 2 days.

Flowerpaste (gum paste)

This hard-setting paste can be formed into many shapes and designs.

8tsp warm water
2tsp powdered gelatine
500g (1lb/4cups) icing (confectioners') sugar
4tsp gum tragacanth
2tsp liquid glucose
15g (1tbsp) white vegetable fat (shortening)
2tbsp plus 1tsp egg white (fresh or albumen powder)

1 Measure the water into a small dish and sprinkle over the gelatine. Leave to soak for 1 hour.

2 Sift the icing (confectioners') sugar and gum tragacanth into the bowl of an electric mixer and warm gently.

3 Dissolve the gelatine mixture over a pan of hot water, add the liquid glucose and vegetable fat. Stir until dissolved.

4 Place the bowl of icing sugar and gum tragacanth on the electric mixer. Add the gelatine mixture and egg white and beat for 5 minutes until white and stringy.

Store in a plastic bag inside an airtight container in the refrigerator for 24 hours before use. When removed, knead it with lightly greased hands until soft.

Pastillage

This alternative to flowerpaste (gum paste) can be used immediately.

1½tsp powdered gelatine
4tbsp water
½tsp gum tragacanth
500g (1lb/4cups) icing (confectioners') sugar

1 Sprinkle the gelatine on the water and leave to soften. Sift the gum tragacanth and sugar into a bowl and warm gently.

2 Dissolve the gelatine over hot water. Add the gelatine to the sugar mixture and beat on a slow speed with an electric mixer for about 3 minutes.

Refrigerate in an airtight container.

Modelling paste

Modelling paste is a half-and-half mix of flowerpaste (gum paste) and sugarpaste (rolled fondant) used to make models.

Lining cake tins

There is nothing more disappointing after carefully mixing and baking a cake than to open the oven door and find that your cake is misshapen. However, if you put a little extra time and effort into the preparation of the tins (pans), your cakes should be perfectly shaped.

Choosing the cake tin (pan)

Choose and prepare the cake tin well before you make the mixture. Cake tins not only come in the round and square type traditionally used at Christmas time but also in the shape of bells, flowers, hearts and diamonds. Many tins are aluminium, but some are made of tin, specially treated to make them non-stick and food safe. The size of tins given in recipes is for the measurement across the base. If you want to use a different tin from that stated, you will need to use a tin with the same capacity. So, if the recipe asks for a 20cm (8in) round cake tin, fill a tin this size with water, then gradually transfer the water into the chosen tin, until it is full. In this way, you can work out how many quantities of mixture are required to fill the tin.

How much lining?

Average-sized cakes or fruit cakes that are not in the oven for extended cooking times only require a single layer of greaseproof (parchment) paper to line the base and sides. However, larger cakes or those that require long cooking times (most fruit cakes) will need extra protection from burning, both around the side and under the base of the tin.

Successful lining

Lightly grease the tin with melted butter or a mild-flavoured vegetable oil.

Cut a double layer of paper into a strip long enough to fit around the outside of the tin and tall enough to come about 5cm (2in) above the edge of the tin. Fold down a cuff about 2cm (¾in) deep along the length of the strip, along the folded edges.

Make diagonal cuts up to the fold line on each strip about 1cm (½in) apart. Fit the strip around the inside of the tin, with the cuts on the base, pressing the cuts out at right angles so they sit flat around the base. Place the tin on a doubled piece of greaseproof (parchment) paper and draw around the edge. Cut the shape and place on the base of the tin, over the cuts.

Before turning on the oven, prepare the tin following these instructions and have the oven shelves in the correct position to accommodate the lined tin. Cakes are normally cooked on the third shelf.

Spoon the mixture into the tin, ensuring it is pushed well into corners and edges. Tap the tin on your working area to remove any air bubbles. Smooth the top with fingers dipped in water. Decorate the top with fruit or nuts if desired. To prevent the cake burning on the outside, fold over sheets of newspaper long enough to wrap around the side of the tin and to come a little higher than the greaseproof paper. Tie around the tin securely with string and sit the tin on several layers of folded newspaper on the oven shelf. The oven temperature is low enough to use paper safely.

When the cake is cold, remove it from the tin, then remove the paper. If there is a wet spot on the base of the cake, return the cake to the tin and cook for another hour, or until dried out. If the edges and side of the cake feel a little dry, brush all over with brandy or rum and wrap in clingfilm (plastic wrap). Store in an airtight container.

Gâteau tiramisu

Tiramisu means 'pick-me-up' in Italian and that is certainly what this cake will do during the Christmas season. It is rich and creamy, flavoured with a coffee syrup made from Kahlua, and layered with mascarpone cream.

Cake and decoration

2 x 23cm (9in) genoese sponges (see page 10)
1tbsp instant coffee powder or granules
200g (6½oz/¾cup) caster (superfine) sugar
80ml (2¾floz/⅓cup) Kahlua
4 egg yolks
500g (1lb) mascarpone cheese
300ml (10floz/1¼cups) thick cream
Cocoa powder
500g (1lb) chocolate cream wafers or chocolate curls (long thin cigar shapes)
Brown or Christmas-patterned ribbon

Equipment

Electric mixer
Paintbrushes

1 Combine the coffee powder and 110g (3½oz/½cup) of the caster (superfine) sugar in a small pan with 250ml (8floz/1cup) water. Stir the mixture over a low heat until the sugar has completely dissolved. Remove from the heat and leave to cool slightly, then stir in the Kahlua.

2 Add the egg yolks and the remaining caster sugar to a heatproof bowl and place the bowl over a pan of barely simmering water. Beat the yolks and sugar for 3 minutes using electric beaters, or until the mixture has turned thick and fluffy and leaves a trail on its surface. Remove from the heat and transfer to a cool, clean bowl. Beat for 3 minutes, or until cool.

3 Gently stir the mascarpone cheese in a large bowl to soften it. Add the egg yolk mixture, followed by the cream, and then beat the ingredients together slightly until thick.

4 Take the two genoese sponge cakes and slice them both in half horizontally. Place a layer of cake on a serving plate or board and generously brush over the surface with the coffee syrup. Spread with about a fifth of the mascarpone cream. Top with another round of cake and continue layering with the syrup, mascarpone cream and cake, finishing with a layer of mascarpone cream. Refrigerate the cake and the remaining portion of filling for 1 hour.

5 Dust the top of the cake liberally with cocoa powder and spread the remaining mascarpone cream around the side. Trim the chocolate wafers to stand a little higher than the cake and press them gently side-by-side around

Build up the layers of cake, brushed with coffee syrup and mascarpone cream.

the cake. Tie the ribbon around the cake and fasten it with a large bow.

Ahead of time: This cake can be stored for a day, covered, in the refrigerator. Do not decorate with the wafers until ready to serve as they will soften if left to stand.

Trim the chocolate wafers to size and arrange them around the edge of the cake.

Fresh fruit mince tarts

Mince tarts are perfect to give away as presents to friends and family. Prepare a couple of batches of these home-made goodies to cater for any unexpected guest! They will also look – and smell – great as the centrepiece of your table. This recipe makes 24 small tarts.

For the pastry

200g (7oz/1¾cups) plain
(all-purpose) flour
150g (5oz/⅔cup) butter, chopped
80g (2¾oz/¾cup) ground hazelnuts
2tbsp caster (superfine) sugar
1–2 tbsp iced water
Icing (confectioners') sugar

For the filling

125g (4oz/¾cup) blueberries
200g (6½oz/1cup) peeled, finely
chopped apple
80g (2¾oz/½cup) raisins, chopped
75g (2½oz/½cup) currants
80g (2¾oz/½cup) sultanas
(golden raisins)
30g (1oz/¼cup) slivered
almonds, toasted
60g (2oz/¼cup) caster
(superfine) sugar
2tbsp mixed peel
125ml (4floz/½cup) brandy
1tsp grated lemon rind
½tsp mixed spice
½tsp ground ginger

Equipment

Flat-bladed knife
7cm (2¾in) round cutter
2 deep, 12-hole tartlet pans
4.5cm (1¾in) star cutter

1 To make the pastry, sift the flour into a large bowl and rub in the butter with your fingers to form breadcrumbs. Stir in the nuts and sugar. Make a well and mix in the water with a flat-bladed knife until the mixture comes together in beads. Make balls of dough and place onto a lightly floured surface. Flatten slightly into a disc. Cover with clingfilm (plastic wrap) and leave for 30 minutes.

Mix the pastry with a knife until the mixture comes together in beads.

2 Preheat the oven to 180°C/ 350°F/ gas mark 4. Roll out the dough to a 3mm (⅛in) thickness on greaseproof (parchment) paper. Cut 24 round shapes with the cutter and fit into the holes of the tartlet pans. Line with greaseproof paper and fill with baking beads. Bake for 10 minutes, remove the paper and beads and bake for another 10 minutes.

3 Gather together the pastry scraps and roll to a 3mm (⅛in) thickness. Using the 4.5cm (1¾in) star cutter, cut 24 shapes from the pastry for the tart lids. If preferred, you can use bell- or holly-shaped cutters.

4 To make the filling, place all the ingredients in a saucepan and simmer, stirring, for 5 to 10 minutes, or until the mixture is thick and pulpy. Allow to cool slightly. Then, divide the mixture among the pastry cases, and top each with a pastry lid. Bake for approximately 20 minutes, or until the lids are golden. Leave in the pans for about 5 minutes before transferring to a wire rack to cool. Dust with sifted icing (confectioners') sugar before serving.

Place a pastry shape on top of each tart before baking.

Glacé-topped fruit cake

This recipe is very simple, but will let you dress up a simple rich fruit cake into something special. Why not try the variation to make 12 individual-sized cakes and serve each guest with a miniature dessert?

Cake and decoration

1 unbaked fruit cake mixture
(see pages 8–9)
750g (1½lb) mixed glacé (candied) fruit, roughly chopped (try a mixture of apricots, pineapple, ginger and cherries)
3tsp gelatine
Decorative ribbon

Equipment

18 x 25cm (7 x 10in) oval cake tin (pan)
Paintbrushes

1 Pre-heat the oven to 150°C/ 300°F/ gas mark 2. Line the base and side of the cake tin (pan) with two layers of brown paper and two layers of non-stick greaseproof (parchment) paper. Wrap three layers of newspaper around the outside of the tin, securing with string.

2 Spoon the cake mixture into the tin and smooth the surface with wet fingertips. Tap the tin several times to remove any air bubbles from the mixture. Place in the oven on top of several layers of newspaper and bake for 3 hours, then arrange the glacé (candied) fruit over the top. Bake for a further 30 minutes, then cover loosely with creased foil or greaseproof paper to prevent the fruit from burning. Bake for another hour, or until a skewer comes out clean when inserted into the centre of the fruit cake.

3 Put 2 tablespoons of boiling water in a bowl and sprinkle with the gelatine. Leave for 1 minute until spongy, then stir briskly with a fork to dissolve. Brush the gelatine over the hot cake, cover the top with greaseproof paper and wrap in a tea (kitchen) towel. Allow to cool in the tin, then turn out and tie the ribbon around the cake.

Ahead of time: This cake is perfect for making in advance – wrapped tightly in clingfilm (plastic wrap), it can be stored in an airtight container for up to a year.

Variation: This recipe can also be made as small, individual cakes.

Lightly grease a 12-hole 250ml (8floz/1cup) muffin tin (pan) with melted butter or mild-flavoured oil and fit a circle of greaseproof paper in the bottom of each hole.

Spoon in the cake mixture and smooth the surface with wet fingertips. Top with the glacé fruit and bake for 1¼ hours, or until a skewer comes out clean when inserted into the centre of the cakes. Remove from the oven and proceed as instructed for the large fruit cake.

Dip your hand in water and use to smooth the top of the cake mixture.

Dissolve the gelatine in boiling water and brush over the glacé fruit.

Christmas trees

This unusual Christmas cake uses simple jabot-style folded frills to decorate the top of the cake. Shaped like Christmas trees, they are edged with delicate piping. The side of the cake is decorated with a delicate wreath of holly leaves, cones and berries.

Cake and decoration

20 x 25cm (8 x 10in) scalloped, oval fruit cake (see pages 8–9)
28 x 33cm (11 x 13in) scalloped, oval cake board
1.5kg (3lb) marzipan (almond icing)
2kg (4lb) sugarpaste (rolled fondant)
Small quantity of royal icing
Edible glue
Green, gold and red ribbons
18 large and 18 small silk or sugar holly leaves
6 silk or sugar fir cones
24 silk or sugar holly berries
60g (2oz) modelling paste
Red, green and gold food colourings

Equipment

Scriber
Paintbrushes
Small star cutter
Set of ring cutters
Frilling tool
Piping bags (cones)
2 no.0 plain piping tubes (tips)

1 Marzipan (almond ice) the cake, then cover the cake and board with sugarpaste (rolled fondant) (see pages 12–13). Allow to dry for at least 3 days. Secure the cake to the board with royal icing (see pages 14–15).

2 Scribe a line around the sides of the cake 2.5cm (1in) up from the base and, using edible glue, attach a length of green ribbon along this line. Attach another length, 1cm (½in) above the first. Secure the gold ribbon around the base of the cake. Trim the board with the red and green ribbons.

3 At regular intervals around the cake, just above the green ribbons, attach the large holly leaves with icing. Attach the small leaves, cones and berries. Reserve three leaves and three berries.

4 To make the stars, roll out some modelling paste (see page 15) and cut out 30 small stars. Leave eight to dry and attach the rest with edible glue to the board. Paint the eight stars gold.

5 To make the trees, roll out more modelling paste and cut two 10cm (4in) circles and one 7.5cm (3in) circle with ring cutters. Cut a 4cm (1½in) centre in each circle. With a frilling tool, soften around the outer edge. Cut through the frill to form a strip. Fold one end under. Repeat, working from side to side until you get a fluted cone. Once dry, attach to the top of the cake with royal icing. Colour some royal icing red and green and fill two bags (cones) fitted with no.0 tubes (tips). Pipe green dots around the edges of the frills and fill with red dots.

6 Attach the reserved holly leaves and berries to either side of the top of the cake, and the gold stars above the trees. Make small rectangles from modelling paste and use to form the tree trunks.

Secure the small holly leaves, cones and berries with a little royal icing.

Pipe green and red dots around the edges of the frill to form a continuous border.

Christmas wreath

Use a rich fruit cake recipe and you can do your baking and decorating up to 2 months before Christmas and rest assured that your cake will taste even better than the day it came out of the oven.

Cake and decoration

23cm (9in) round fruit cake
(see pages 8–9)
400g (13oz) marzipan (almond icing)
500g (1lb/4cups) icing
(confectioners') sugar
3 egg whites, lightly beaten
25cm (10in) round cake board
Small quantity of royal icing
200g (6½oz) sugarpaste (rolled fondant)
Green and red food colourings
Decorative ribbon

Equipment

Electric hand mixer
Palette knife
Steel ruler
Leaf-shaped cutters
Paintbrushes

1 Marzipan (almond ice) the cake (see page 12) and leave to dry overnight.

2 Sift the icing (confectioners') sugar into a large bowl, making sure there are no lumps. Make a well in the centre and add the egg whites, stirring from the centre outwards until completely mixed in. The mixture will be fairly stiff. Beat with an electric hand mixer until you obtain a fluffy consistency – the icing should be spreadable but not runny.

3 Secure the cake to the cake board with a little royal icing (see pages 14–15). Spoon about a third of the icing on top and spread out to the edge of the cake with a palette knife. Use a steel ruler to smooth the surface of the cake. Ice the side of the cake. If possible, use a turntable to ease the icing process. Otherwise, place the cake board on top of the upturned cake tin that you have just used, to give you a little more height and make turning the cake easier. When you have as smooth a surface as possible, leave the cake to dry. (To create a snow scene, use the end of the palette knife to press down and lift at intervals all over the icing to make peaks.) Make sure to keep a little icing, covered with clingfilm (plastic wrap).

4 Roll out the sugarpaste (rolled fondant) (see page 13) on a clean work surface that has been dusted with icing sugar and cut out leaf shapes with the cutters. Leave to dry thoroughly, either flat or over a rolling pin to make them curve slightly. Then, paint them different shades of green. Roll a few holly berries and paint them red when dry.

5 Decorate the cake with a wreath of leaves, attaching each one with a little icing, and add a few berries. Tie with the decorative ribbon. Dust lightly with icing sugar to serve.

Ahead of time: The decorated cake can be stored for 2 months in an airtight container in a cool place.

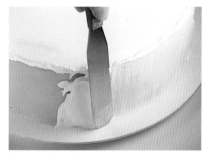

A turntable will make it easier to ice the cake, or place the cake on top of the tin.

Leaf cutters are a good investment as they give a really neat finish.

Christmas bell

Ring out the times of Christmas cheer! This traditionally decorated bell is enhanced with a poinsettia, Christmas roses and ivy leaves. You can choose to make the flowers yourself, using flowerpaste (gum paste), or use silk flowers for an easier option.

Cake and decoration

Ready-made, large bell-shaped fruit cake (see pages 8–9)
1kg (2lb) marzipan (almond icing)
28cm (11in) round cake board
1.25kg (2½lb) white sugarpaste (rolled fondant)
Small quantity of royal icing
Silk or sugar poinsettias
Silk or sugar Christmas roses with leaves
Decorative ribbon

Equipment

Closed-curve crimpers
Piping bag (cone)
No.1.5 piping tube (tip)
Posy pick
Endless Garrett frill cutter
Paintbrush
26g green and white wires

1 Marzipan (almond ice) the bell cake, leave to dry thoroughly, then cover the cake and the board with sugarpaste (rolled fondant) (see pages 12–13). Crimp the outer edge of the board.

2 Fit a piping bag (cone) with a no.1.5 tube (tip) and fill with royal icing (see pages 14–15). Pipe a small snail trail around the base of the cake. Then, place a posy pick at the top of the cake, while the sugarpaste is still soft so the paste does not crack.

3 Divide the base of the bell into six and mark the sections with a dot of icing to indicate the position of the Garrett frills.

4 Roll out a thin strip of sugarpaste and, with a Garrett frill cutter, cut one long frill. Then, roll the end of a paintbrush across the scalloped edge. Dampen the top, unscalloped edge of the frill with a little water. Attach this edge from dot to dot around the bell, using the brush to raise the scalloped edge at intervals.

5 Cut out a second frill and repeat the procedure, placing this second frill just above the first one. Then, pipe a small snail trail around the top of the frill. Finally, pipe a random pattern of seven dots all over the bell.

6 Decorate the bell with silk or sugar poinsettias and Christmas roses (see step 5, page 72). Secure the flowers and leaves in the posy pick on top of the bell.

7 Position five strands of your chosen ribbon to trail delicately down the bell.

Attach a matching ribbon around the board then, just at the top of each frill, add a small blossom and two leaves either side.

Note: Ready-made bell cakes are available in most cake decorating shops.

If preferred, make your own Christmas roses using flowerpaste (gum paste).

If you are making your own poinsettias, use readily available poinsettia cutters.

Chocolate leaf cake

This cake is simple to make and also fun, especially if you have children who enjoy helping out in the kitchen at Christmas time. What better way to spend a winter afternoon than painting leaves with chocolate?

Cake and decoration

250g (8oz) dark chocolate, chopped
125ml (4floz/½cup) cream
2tsp glycerine
2tsp golden (corn) syrup
20cm (8in) round chocolate mud cake
(see page 10)
90g (3oz) white chocolate drops
90g (3oz) milk chocolate drops
90g (3oz) dark chocolate drops
Assorted non-toxic leaves
(such as rose leaves)

Equipment

Serrated knife
Paintbrushes
Small piping bag (cone)

1 To make the dark chocolate glaze, combine the chocolate, cream, glycerine and golden syrup in a heatproof bowl. Bring a small pan of water to simmer, remove from the heat and place the bowl over the pan to melt the mixture. Stir over the hot water until the glaze is smooth. Or, melt in the microwave for 30 seconds on a high setting.

2 Using a serrated knife, cut the domed top off the cake to give a flat surface. Turn the cake upside down on a wire rack so that the flat base becomes the top. Stand the wire rack over a tray to catch any glaze that may drip. Pour the glaze over the top of the cake and allow it to run evenly down the sides of the cake, completely coating it. Tap the tray on your work surface to give a level

surface. Refrigerate for up to 15 minutes to let the glaze set.

3 Line two oven trays with greaseproof (parchment) paper. Melt the white, milk and dark chocolate drops in separate heatproof bowls. Bring a small pan of water to a simmer, remove from the heat and place the bowl over the pan, ensuring the base of the bowl does not touch the water. Stir the chocolate over the hot water until melted. Or, melt in the microwave for 1 minute on a high setting, stirring after 30 seconds.

4 Make sure your leaves are clean and dry. Brush chocolate over one side of each leaf, using different coloured chocolates on some of the leaves and brushing some on the smooth side and some on the vein side. Always coat more leaves than are needed in case some break. Place the leaves on lined trays to dry. Spoon a little of the dark chocolate into the piping bag (cone), snip off the end and pipe twigs onto one of the trays. Leave to set.

5 Carefully peel the leaves away from the chocolate. Put the cake on a serving plate or stand and pile the leaves and twigs on top.

Spoon some of the dark chocolate into a piping bag to make twigs.

Once the chocolate has set, carefully peel away the leaves.

Parcel cake

For a truly spectacular design, inspire yourself from patterns on existing Christmas wrapping paper. You can use coloured sugarpaste (rolled fondant) of your choice, so why not innovate with a stunning red cake?

Cake and decoration

20cm (8in) round cake of your choice
(see pages 8–11)
25cm (10in) cake board
1kg (2lb) marzipan (almond icing)
1kg (2lb) sugarpaste
(rolled fondant)
Red, green and pale blue
food colourings
Silver non-toxic paint
Red ribbon
Edible glue
Small quantity of white royal icing
(optional)

Equipment

Rolling pin
Christmas tree cutters in a variety
of sizes
No.0 paintbrush
Piping bags (cones) (optional)
No.0 piping tube (tip) (optional)

1 Cover the cake with marzipan (almond icing) (see page 12) and place on the centre of the board.

2 Prepare the sugarpaste (rolled fondant) (see page 13) to cover the cake, rolling it out to the desired size and shape. Cover with clingfilm (plastic wrap) so the paste does not dry out.

Place the cut-out shapes on the white sugarpaste then roll once with a rolling pin.

3 Reserve a small amount of the remaining sugarpaste and colour it red, then colour half the remaining paste pale blue and the other half green. Roll out the blue and green pastes separately. Cut out Christmas trees in various sizes from both colour pastes using the cutters. The trees to be painted silver are better cut from very pale blue paste as this will not affect the colour of the silver when it is applied. Make sure the cut edges are well defined as the overall effect will be spoilt if the shapes are indistinct or damaged. Use a simple design as speed is essential. Make small balls in red paste and place at random over the trees.

4 Remove the clingfilm from the white sugarpaste and place the tree shapes

onto it. Lay a sheet of greaseproof (parchment) paper over the entire area and roll firmly once using the rolling pin. Lay the paste over the cake. When the sugarpaste is dry and firm, paint the blue trees silver with a no.0 paintbrush.

5 To create the parcel effect, place two pieces of red ribbon across the cake and top with a large ribbon rosette. Secure with sugarpaste glue. Attach another length of the ribbon around the board. If desired, pipe a delicate snail trail around the base of the cake for an attractive finish.

Variation: Use a coloured sugarpaste as the base instead of white, and cut out different-coloured tree shapes to create your personal version of this cake.

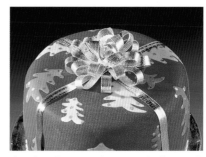

If preferred, use a red paste as the base and decorate with a sparkling silver ribbon.

Individual Christmas cakes

These cute miniature cakes make wonderful Christmas gifts. They can be kept for up to a month after icing, so pack them up in tiny decorated boxes and hand them out to friends and family at Yuletide.

Cake and decoration

1 unbaked fruit cake mixture
(see pages 8–9)
60g (2oz) marzipan (almond icing)
Green and red food colourings
100g (3½oz/⅓cup) apricot jam (jelly)
100g (3½oz) sugarpaste (rolled fondant)
per cake
Decorative ribbon
Small quantity of royal icing
1 egg white
250g (8oz/2cups) icing (confectioners')
sugar, sifted plus a small quantity
to dust
2–3tsp lemon juice

Equipment

12-hole 250ml (8floz/1cup)
muffin tin (pan)
Small holly leaf cutter
Paintbrushes
Palette knife

1 Preheat the oven to 150°C/ 300°F/ gas mark 2. Lightly grease the muffin tin (pan) and line the bases with a circle of greaseproof (parchment) paper. Pour in the cake mixture to the top of the holes and smooth the surface. Bake for 1¼ hours, or until a skewer comes out clean. Leave to cool in the tin before turning out onto a clean surface.

Paint the edges of the leaves with green colouring – not too much or it will bleed.

Spread royal icing smoothly over the top, letting it drizzle down the side.

2 To make the holly leaves, knead 50g (1¾oz) of the marzipan (almond icing) until soft. Roll out very thinly on a surface lightly dusted with icing (confectioners') sugar. Cut out the leaves with the cutter. Pinch the leaves in half, open out and press the edges gently to curl in different directions. Leave to dry, then brush green colouring around the edge of each leaf.

3 Knead a little red colouring into the remaining marzipan and roll out small balls to make berries. Paint or roll the berries through the colouring to coat thoroughly. Leave to dry.

4 To make the cakes covered with sugarpaste (rolled fondant) (see page 13), melt the jam (jelly) until runny, strain and brush over the cakes. Roll out the paste, for one cake at a time, on a surface lightly coated with icing sugar. Fill any holes with a little extra paste. Cover the cake with the paste, easing over the side and pressing lightly. Trim at the base. Wrap the ribbon around the base and seal with a little royal icing (see pages 14–15).

5 To make the royal icing covering, lightly beat the egg white with a wooden spoon. Gradually add the icing sugar, beating to a smooth paste. Slowly add the lemon juice until slightly runny. Spread a tablespoon of icing over each cake. Smooth with a palette knife and let some drizzle down the sides. Leave to dry. Secure the holly leaves and berries to the cake with leftover icing.

Nine-square sparkle

This simple design using cut-outs illustrates many of the traditional objects we associate with Christmas. The crisp white and blue colour scheme adds a contemporary feel, though you could choose a more traditional red and green colour scheme if preferred.

Cake and decoration

20cm (8in) square fruit cake
(see pages 8–9)
1kg (2lb) marzipan (almond icing)
1kg (2lb) white sugarpaste
(rolled fondant)
60g (2oz) flowerpaste (gum paste)
Blue and green paste food colourings
28cm (11in) square cake board
plus 2 spare
Mother-of-pearl, silver snow and disco green dusting powders (petal dusts)
Small quantity of royal icing
Silver dragées
Small quantity of vegetable fat
Cornflour (cornstarch)
Painting solution
Edible glue
Silver ribbon

Equipment

18cm (7½in) square stencil card
Scriber or pin
Ruler
Designer wheel
Bobble tool
Templates (see page 93) and craft knife
Paintbrushes

1 Divide the stencil card into nine 6cm (2½in) squares. Cut a small V shape in the edge of each division.

2 Marzipan (almond ice) the cake, then cover with sugarpaste (rolled fondant) (see pages 12–13). Reserve the excess.

3 While the sugarpaste is still soft, place the stencil on top of the cake. Mark the dividing lines with a scriber or pin. Remove the stencil and impress lines across the sugarpaste with a ruler, using the scribed lines as guides. Use a designer wheel to indent 'stitches' along the dividing lines. Let the paste dry.

4 Colour two-thirds of the flowerpaste (gum paste) (see page 15) pale blue. Add green to half the blue paste to make turquoise. Colour the reserved sugarpaste turquoise, roll out and cut in strips. Use to cover the cake board. Roll a bobble tool over the surface to texture.

Brush with mother-of-pearl dusting powder (petal dust).

5 Secure the silver dragées to the cake with royal icing (see pages 14–15).

6 Coat two boards with vegetable fat and roll out the two flowerpastes very thinly. Transfer to a surface dusted with cornflour (cornstarch). Trace the templates and cut out the shapes from sugarpaste, using a combination of the two colours. Mix silver snow dusting powder with painting solution and highlight areas on them. Brush them with mother-of-pearl and secure to the cake with edible glue. Sprinkle disco green over the decorations and along the turquoise board. Finally, attach the silver ribbon to the board.

Place the template on top of the cake and mark the dividing points with a scriber.

Remove the template and impress lines across the sugarpaste with a ruler.

Poinsettia tree

The rich, deep red and green colours of this stylish tree cake will add a festive touch to your Christmas table. For an easier option, you could buy silk or sugar poinsettias instead of making them yourself.

Cake and decoration

25 x 20cm (10 x 8in) shallow
sponge cake (see pages 10–11)
Buttercream or jam (jelly) for filling
and masking
375g (12oz) moss green sugarpaste
(rolled fondant)
Triangular cake board
75g (2½oz) red pastillage
7g (¼oz) yellowy-green sugarpaste
(rolled fondant)
1 small and 2 medium sprigs of artificial
holly leaves and berries
5 artificial spruce sprigs
10 gold dragées
Gold cardboard star
Tartan ribbon bow
30g (1oz/¼cup) royal icing

Equipment

Ribbed rolling pin
Large holly leaf cutter
Paintbrush

1 Cut the cake as shown and join the pieces with buttercream or jam (jelly) to make a triangle. Mask the top and sides with buttercream. Roll out the green sugarpaste (rolled fondant) and cover the cake (see page 13). Texture the top with the ribbed rolling pin and trim off the excess paste. Place on the board.

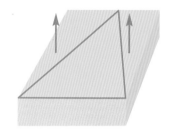

Cover the cake with green sugarpaste and texture the surface with a ribbed rolling pin.

2 Roll out the red pastillage (see page 15) and cut out several holly leaf shapes for the petals. If you wish, mark veins using the back of a knife.

3 Make a short rope of green sugarpaste and attach to the top of the cake with a little water to form a ring. Attach a small ball of paste in the centre. Arrange the red petals in two layers, securing them with a little water. Roll small balls of the yellowy-green sugarpaste, indent slightly with the handle of a paintbrush and attach to the centre of the flower.

4 Arrange the dragées, gold star, tartan bow and sprigs of holly and spruce attractively on the cake and attach with a little royal icing (see pages 14–15).

Cut a triangle shape and lift up the sides.

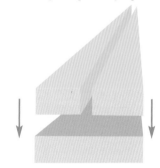

Flip the two sides and join together.

Cut poinsettia leaves out of the red pastillage using a large holly leaf cutter.

Blue angel cake

Blue and silver is a perfect alternative to the more traditional red and green colour scheme. In this particular creation, the white angel is made in half-relief, and is enhanced by an array of glittering stars.

Cake and decoration

23cm (9in) round fruit cake
(see pages 8–9)
750g (1½lb) marzipan (almond icing)
30cm (12in) round cake board
750g (1½lb) baby blue sugarpaste
(rolled fondant)
125g (4oz) white flowerpaste
(gum paste)
Chestnut brown and autumn leaf
food colourings
Small quantity of royal icing
Edible glue
Edible glitter
Decorative ribbon

Equipment

Closed curve crimpers
Templates (see page 92)
Paintbrushes
Textured rolling pin
Ball tool
Small straw
Palette knife
Dresden tool
Large and small star cutters

1 Marzipan (almond ice) the cake, place it on the board, then cover both with sugarpaste (rolled fondant) (see pages 12–13). Crimp the edge of the board.

Assemble the angel on a flat surface before placing it onto the cake.

2 Trace the templates to form an attractive design for the angel. Place it in a plastic bag and use it as a guide to build up the head and body using flowerpaste (gum paste) (see page 15). Indent the features onto the face, then paint the eyes and mouth chestnut brown. Paint the hair with autumn leaf.

3 Roll out the flowerpaste and cut out shapes for the dress. Texture with the rolling pin. Gather each piece at the waist. Cut out and texture the bodice. With a ball tool, make an indentation for the arm. Lift the angel onto the cake with a palette knife. Secure with royal icing (see pages 14–15).

4 Make a small, tapered strip of flowerpaste. At the small end, form an oval shape for the hand and cut small V shapes for the fingers and thumb. Form the wrist by rolling between two fingers, then gently bend the arm at the elbow. Place the upper arm into the indent. Secure with royal icing and leave to dry.

5 Roll out more paste and cut two wing shapes. Vein the top of the wings with a small straw then, with a dresden tool, draw lines for long feathers. Ball the outer edges. Place onto the angel, securing with royal icing. Allow to dry.

6 Cut out small flowerpaste stars, allow to dry, then paint one side with edible glue. Dip into the glitter. Leave to dry then secure on the cake with royal icing. Repeat for the large star. Attach the ribbon to the cake board.

Paint one side of the stars with edible glue, then dip them into edible glitter.

Christmas frosted fruits

For something a little different at Christmas time, sugar coat a collection of berries, currants and tiny stone fruit and pile them high on this traditional fruit cake. Use a combination of light and dark fruit.

Cake and decoration

Selection of seasonal fruits such as white and dark cherries, red or white currants, blackcurrants, apricots or tiny plums
1 egg white
Caster (superfine) sugar
1 egg white
1–3tsp lemon juice
125g (4oz/1cup) icing (confectioners') sugar, sifted
18 x 25cm (7 x 10in) oval fruit cake (see pages 8–9)

Equipment

Paintbrush
Palette knife

1 Wash the fruit and make sure it is dry before starting the coating process. If possible, wash it beforehand and leave to dry for several hours.

2 Line a tray with paper towel. Place the egg white in a shallow bowl and whisk until just foamy. Put some caster (superfine) sugar on a large plate. Work with one piece of fruit at a time, except for the berries, which can be sugared in small bunches. Brush the egg white lightly over the fruit, making sure the entire piece of fruit is covered – but not too heavily.

Paint the fruit with a little egg white, then sprinkle with the caster sugar.

3 Sprinkle the caster sugar over the fruit and shake off any excess, then leave on the tray to dry thoroughly. The drying time will depend on the surrounding humidity. Always frost more fruit than you need so you have a good selection to choose from when arranging.

Smooth the icing over the cake, allowing it to run slowly down the side.

4 To make the top icing, whisk the remaining egg white until you obtain a consistency that is just foamy. Beat in 1 teaspoon of the lemon juice. Add the icing (confectioners') sugar gradually, beating well after each addition. The icing should be quite thick and white – add a little more lemon juice if necessary, making sure the mixture does not become too runny.

5 Place the fruit cake on a serving plate or stand. Working very quickly, pour the icing over the top. Using a palette knife, carefully smooth the icing to the edge of the cake, allowing it to run slowly down the side. Leave the cake for about 10 minutes to let the icing set a little.

6 Arrange the frosted fruits decoratively on top of the cake. Make sure to mix the light-coloured fruit with the darker ones for a more dramatic effect.

Ahead of time: The fruits can be frosted several hours in advance.

Stencil cake

This deliciously rich mud cake is one for the budding artists in the kitchen. Making your own stencil is as easy or as difficult as you want it to be – you can let your imagination run wild for a dramatic design or create a simpler but equally attractive decoration.

Cake and decoration

23cm (9in) square chocolate mud cake (see page 10)
Cake board or serving plate
90g (3oz) dark chocolate, chopped
150g (5oz/²⁄₃cup) unsalted butter
2tbsp icing (confectioners') sugar
Dark cocoa powder
Chocolate sticks

Equipment

Sheet of cardboard
Serrated knife
Craft knife or sharp scissors
Electric mixer
Palette knife

1 Put the chocolate cake on the piece of cardboard and draw around the outside to make an outline. Using a serrated knife, cut the domed top of the cake to leave a flat surface. If you wish, trim the sides of the cake to make a very even, sharp-edged square. Turn the cake upside down on a cake board or serving plate, so that the flat base of the cake becomes the top.

2 Draw the design of your choice on the cardboard and cut out with a craft knife or sharp scissors. Use firm board so that the stencil is not too floppy.

3 To make the chocolate buttercream, bring a pan containing a little water to a simmer. Put the dark chocolate in a heatproof bowl. Remove the pan from the heat and place the bowl over the pan, making sure not to let the base of the bowl sit in the water. Stir the chocolate until melted. Then, beat the butter with electric beaters until light and creamy. Gradually beat in the cooled, melted chocolate and the icing (confectioners') sugar. Continue beating until the mixture becomes pale and creamy. Spread the buttercream evenly over the top and sides of the cake, smoothing the surface as cleanly as possible with a palette knife. Place the cake in the refrigerator for about 30 minutes, or until the buttercream becomes quite firm.

Cut the cardboard to the same size as the cake, draw on a design and cut out.

Place the stencil over the top of the cake and shake the cocoa powder over it.

4 Gently place the stencil over the top of the cake. Place a small amount of cocoa powder in a fine sieve. Carefully lift the stencil off the cake without spilling any cocoa that is still on the cardboard. Press the chocolate sticks, upright, around the side of the cake – if they are too long, or uneven, trim them all so they stand just a little higher than the top of the cake.

Ahead of time: The cake can be decorated up to 2 days in advance. Store in the refrigerator in warm weather, or in an airtight container in a cool, dry place.

The last Christmas post

Even with careful planning, there are always last-minute Christmas cards to be posted! Instructions to make the gorgeous robins are given but, if you are a sugarcraft novice, you can always use ready-made sugar ones.

Cake and decoration

Three 10cm (4in) round fruit cakes
(see pages 8–9)
750g (1½lb) marzipan (almond icing)
1kg (2lb) poppy red sugarpaste
(rolled fondant)
25cm (10in) round cake board
13cm (5in) thin, round board
Small quantity of royal icing
100g (3½oz) black sugarpaste
(rolled fondant)
500g (1lb) white sugarpaste
(rolled fondant)
Granulated sugar
60g (2oz) modelling paste
60g (2oz) flowerpaste (gum paste)
Brown, red and tangerine dusting
powders (petal dusts)
Black and white paste food colourings
Decorative ribbon

Equipment

Paintbrush
Piping bags (cones)
No.1.5 piping tube (tip)
Templates (see page 94) and craft knife
26g white wires
Dresden tool

1 Stack the three cakes onto the round cake board. Marzipan (almond ice) the cakes, then cover them with red sugarpaste (rolled fondant) (see pages 12–13).

2 Mark two lines up the side to hide paste joins. Place a dome of red sugarpaste onto the thin, round board and put on top of the cake. Cut a thick band of red paste and secure under the edge of the board with royal icing (see pages 14–15). Cut a 1cm (½in) thick strip of red paste and emboss it with the back of a paintbrush. Secure it around the edge of the board with a little water.

3 Cut a band of black sugarpaste and place around the base of the cake. Cut a strip for the letter box and surround with red paste. Position on the cake. Cover the board with white paste. Secure a circle of white paste on top of the cake with water. Dampen all surfaces and sprinkle with sugar. Pipe icicles with royal icing around the top edge.

4 Roll out 20g (¾oz) of modelling paste (see page 15) for each bird. Make a large cone then shape the head. Pinch to make a beak. Score all over to give a feathered texture. Indent a hole for both eyes. Use the templates and refer to page 40, step 5, to make to make the tail and wings from flowerpaste (gum paste)

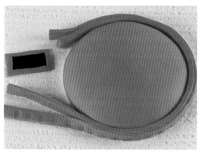

Secure a textured strip of red sugarpaste to the edge of the letter box lid.

(see page 15). Make the feet with wire. Assemble. When dry, dust the top of the body with brown and the chest with red and tangerine. Paint the beak grey with black and white food colouring and the eyes black. Secure in position with icing. Make two small flowerpaste envelopes. Attach the ribbon to the board.

Secure all robin parts together with royal icing, then apply the dusting powders.

Christmas gift

This cake features an attractive holly leaf pattern, very popular around this time of year. To produce this particular effect, brush-embroidery has been used to make both the holly leaves and berries.

Cake and decoration

Two 18cm (7in) round fruit cakes
(see pages 8–9)
28cm (11in) round cake board
1kg (2lb) marzipan (almond icing)
1kg (2lb) sugarpaste (rolled fondant)
Small quantity of royal icing
Christmas green and red food colourings
Red waterproof florists' ribbon

Equipment

No.12 tool (J)
Large holly leaf cutter
Piping bags (cones)
No.1 piping tube (tip)
No.2 paintbrush
Scissors
Large rolling pin

1 Stack the two cakes together and place them on the cake board. Marzipan (almond ice) the cake, then cover both the cake and board with sugarpaste (rolled fondant) (see pages 12–13). Texture the board using a no.12 (Jem) tool, rolling it back and forth.

2 With a large holly leaf cutter, emboss some leaves directly onto the cake in groups of three, leaving a small gap for the berries. Colour some royal icing (see pages 14–15) Christmas green and,

using a no.1 tube (tip), pipe the outer edge of the holly leaves. With a damp brush, work towards the centre of the leaf, creating a central vein. Repeat this all over the cake. Colour the rest of the icing red and pipe in the berries. Flatten the berries with your brush as they are supposed to be wrapping paper designs.

3 Make a 12.5cm (5in) loop of ribbon. Roll around about ten times, then flatten. Cut a point at both ends of the ribbon, leaving the central part of the ribbon intact. Then, put the two centres together and tie with a small piece of ribbon. Open the bow by drawing out from the inside, a loop at a time, alternating from each side. Pull the loops downwards and twist. Repeat with all the loops.

Pipe then paint the holly leaves and berries directly onto the cake.

Use waterproof florists' ribbon to make a decorative bow.

4 Arrange and place the ribbon on the cake with two strips going down at opposite sides of the cake, securing with a little royal icing.

Winter wonderland

This beautiful white cake, depicting a winter snow scene, requires a little time to make but the results are well worth the effort. The simplicity of this creation will provide serenity to your table and festive cheer on a cold, winter's night.

Cake and decoration

Two 18cm (7in) round, light fruit cakes
(see pages 8–9)
4tbsp apricot glaze
33cm (13in) petal silver cake board
1kg (2lb) marzipan (almond icing)
1.5kg (3lb) white sugarpaste
(rolled fondant)
Cornflour (cornstarch)
Small quantity of royal icing
Blue and white dusting powders
(petal dusts)
Icing (confectioners') sugar, sifted

Equipment

Large, soft paintbrush
Templates (see page 94)
Piping bags (cones)
Fine writing tube (tip)
Wooden cocktail sticks (toothpicks)

1 Level off the domes on top of the cakes if excessive. Brush them with apricot glaze and sandwich together. Marzipan (almond ice) the cake (see page 12) and place it on the board.

2 Roll 1kg (2lb) of the sugarpaste (rolled fondant) into a 38cm (15in) circle and cover the cake (see page 13). Position small mounds of sugarpaste on the board around the cake. Roll out the rest

of the paste to a long, curved strip and trim the inner edge. Dampen the base of the cake around the mounds, then lay the strip so the trimmed edge rests against the sides of the cake. Smooth out joins and trim excess paste.

4 Trace five of each tree template onto greaseproof (parchment) paper. Fit a piping bag (cone) with the writing tube (tip) and fill with royal icing (see pages 14–15). Lay a sheet of greaseproof paper over the large template and pipe over the outline. Make 35 more large trees, about 60 medium and 40 small ones.

5 Thin some royal icing with water and place in a piping bag. Snip off a tiny tip. Pipe the icing into the tree outlines, easing the icing into the corners with a cocktail stick (toothpick). Leave to dry.

6 Dust the sides of the cake with the blue and white dusting powders (petal dusts). Make the colour slightly more dense near the base.

7 Pipe dots of icing all over the cake. Peel off the paper lining from the trees. Pipe a line of icing along the straight edge of a tree shape and secure to the

cake. Build up the tree with four more sections. Alternate large and medium trees around the cake. Make standing trees by attaching six or seven sections together. Secure to the board with royal icing. Arrange some in clusters. Place a medium tree on top of the cake. Dust them with icing (confectioners') sugar.

Pipe icing into the tree outlines, easing it into the corners with a cocktail stick.

To assemble the trees, pipe icing along the straight edge and press onto the cake.

Cappuccino truffle cake

Once you have mastered the art of making cappuccino truffles, your Christmas will become a time of true indulgence. You can always make extra truffles and offer them as Christmas gifts in decorative boxes.

Cake and decoration

250ml (8floz/1cup) cream
500g (16½oz) white chocolate drops
Cake board or serving plate
400g (13oz/1⅔cups) unsalted butter
160g (5½oz/1⅓cups) icing
(confectioners') sugar
1tbsp instant coffee powder
Two 23cm (9in) square butter cakes
(or you could use chocolate or coconut
cake, see pages 10–11)
200g (6½oz/1⅓cups) hazelnuts, roasted
and roughly chopped
250g (8oz) dark chocolate, chopped
3tsp Kahlua
2tsp instant coffee powder
16 Ferrero Rocher chocolates
Cocoa powder

1 To make the coffee buttercream, put 170ml (5¼floz/⅔cup) of the cream and 300g (10oz) of the chocolate drops in a small heatproof bowl. Bring a small pan of water to a simmer, remove from the heat and place the bowl over the pan. Do not let the bottom of the bowl sit in the water. Stir over the hot water until melted. Beat the butter until light and creamy, then gradually beat in the sugar until thick and white. Beat in the cooled, melted chocolate until thick and fluffy. Dissolve the instant coffee in a tablespoon of hot water, cool, then beat into the buttercream.

2 Put one cake on a serving plate or board. Spread with a quarter of the buttercream and sandwich with the other cake. Cover with the remaining buttercream. Press the hazelnuts into the side of the cake.

3 To make the chocolate truffles, bring 80ml (2¾floz/⅓cup) of the cream to the boil in a small pan then remove from the heat. Add the dark chocolate and stir until melted. Stir in the Kahlua and coffee. Transfer to a small bowl, cover and refrigerate until cold and thick.

4 Roll rounded teaspoons of the mixture into balls (you should be able to make 25 truffles). Place on a baking tray lined with greaseproof (parchment) paper and leave to firm. If the mixture is too soft to roll, drop rounded teaspoons of mixture onto the tray and refrigerate for about 15 minutes to firm up before rolling into small balls.

5 Melt 200g (6½oz) of the chocolate drops in a heatproof bowl, cool slightly, then use a spoon and fork to dip and coat the truffles in the melted chocolate. Place on a clean piece of greaseproof paper and refrigerate for about 15 minutes to set the chocolate.

6 Pile the truffles and Ferrero Rocher chocolates on top of the cake, using any remaining melted chocolate to hold them in place. Dust with cocoa.

Cover the cake with buttercream and stick the hazelnuts to the sides.

Roll rounded teaspoons of the truffle mixture into balls.

Festive candle wreath

Family and friends will gasp with amazement as you bring this candle wreath lit to the Christmas table. If preferred, replace the Christmas roses with poinsettias. This cake can easily be cut into thin slices.

Cake and decoration

18cm (7in) chocolate sponge ring
(see page 10)
Buttercream for filling and masking
185g (6oz) chocolate sugarpaste
(rolled fondant)
23cm (9in) round gold cake board
Red ribbon
75g (2½oz) green pastillage
45g (1½oz) red pastillage
Orange and brown dusting powders
(petal dusts)
Small quantity of royal icing
Twisted gold candle (optional)
16 gold, foil-wrapped chocolate spheres
or balls
Small quantity of melted chocolate
3 white silk Christmas roses

Equipment

Large holly leaf cutter
Piece of aluminium foil
Paintbrush

1 Cut the chocolate sponge ring in half and sandwich the two halves with buttercream. Mask the surface of the cake with a very thin layer of the same buttercream.

2 Roll out the chocolate sugarpaste (rolled fondant) and cover the cake (see page 13). Trim any excess paste from the base edge, reserving the trimmings. Place the cake on the cake board. Trim the board edge with a red ribbon.

3 Roll out the green pastillage (see page 15) thinly and cut out holly leaves using the cutter. Then, place the leaves on some crumpled aluminium foil and leave until they firm up. Divide the red pastillage into very small pieces and roll into balls to make the berries.

Cover the ring cake with the chocolate sugarpaste and trim off any excess paste.

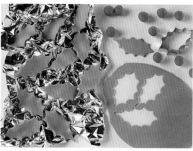

Use a large holly cutter to make leaf shapes and place them on crumpled foil.

4 Tint the holly leaves by brushing with the orange and brown dusting powders (petal dusts). Gather together the sugarpaste trimmings and knead to form a small mound. Place the mound into the centre of the ring, securing it with royal icing (see pages 14–15). If desired, press a candle in position. Attach the foil-wrapped chocolates, leaves and berries to the cake with some melted chocolate. Add the Christmas roses to the centre of the wreath.

Tip: Should you have more time available, you may wish to add more detail to this cake. You can further enhance the decoration shown by introducing red, green or gold ribbon loops and artificial pine cones in between the holly berries.

Star of the show

Chocolate, toffee and truffles – sheer decadence. If you do not have a cake board big enough, you can use a large, clean tile or chopping board. Of course, you can replace the stars with different Christmas designs of your choice.

Cake and decoration

30cm (12in) square, chocolate
mud cake (see page 10)
50 x 40cm (20 x 16in) covered
cake board
500g (1lb) dark chocolate
1kg (2lb/4cups) caster (superfine) sugar
60ml (2floz) brandy
200g (6½oz) dark chocolate, melted
60g (2oz/¼cup) raisins, finely chopped
140g (4½oz/1cup) roasted hazelnuts,
chopped
Dark cocoa powder
Icing (confectioners') sugar

Equipment

Sheet of cardboard
Craft knife or scissors
Large and small star cutters

1 Make a triangular cardboard template, place it on the square cake and cut away the sides of the cake. Place the cake on the board and use part of the sides to build up the top part of the cake into a large triangle. Keep the leftover cake.

2 To make the chocolate glaze, chop the chocolate and put in a pan with 340g (11oz/1½cups) caster (superfine) sugar and 250ml (8floz/1cup) water.

Stir over a low heat until blended. Bring to the boil then reduce the heat slightly. Boil for 6 to 8 minutes, stirring occasionally to prevent burning. Remove from the heat and stir gently to cool. Pour evenly over the cake – do not wash the pan, you will need the leftover glaze. When the glaze has set, trim any drips off the board.

3 To make the chocolate truffles, crumble the reserved cake and measure 900g (1lb 14oz) of cake crumbs into a large bowl. Mix with the brandy, dark chocolate and raisins. Roll into small balls, using 2 level teaspoons for each ball. Roll half the balls in the hazelnuts and the rest in cocoa powder. Refrigerate on greaseproof (parchment) paper-covered trays.

Cut stars out of the template and sprinkle icing sugar through the holes.

Pour the glaze evenly over the cake. When it has set, remove any drips.

4 Cover three oven trays with greaseproof paper. Place a heavy-based frying pan over medium heat, sprinkle with 250g (8oz/1cup) of the caster sugar and, as it melts, gradually sprinkle with the remaining sugar. Stir to melt any lumps. When golden brown, remove from the heat. Pour onto the trays and spread with a wooden spoon. Using a tea (kitchen) towel, tilt the trays to spread the toffee as thinly as possible.

5 When set, break the toffee into jagged pieces and stick to the cake sides with leftover warm glaze. Secure the truffles to the board around the edge of the cake with glaze. Draw around the star cutters on the template and cut the shapes out. Hold the template over the cake and dust with icing (confectioners') sugar.

Christmas bell

A strong design in bright, clear colours gives this bell-shaped cake a very festive feel. Two forms of run-out are used: the top design is flooded directly onto the icing, while the trees and parcels are flooded onto greaseproof (parchment) paper then attached to the cake.

Cake and decoration

25 x 23cm (10 x 9in) flat, bell-shaped butter cake (see page 11)
750g (1½lb) marzipan (almond icing)
1.25kg (2½lb) sugarpaste
(rolled fondant)
36 x 33cm (14 x 13in) bell-shaped cake board
500g (1lb/3¼cups) royal icing
Red, blue, green, yellow, pink and skintone paste food colourings
Piping gel
3 silk or sugar holly leaves
Red ribbon

Equipment

Templates (see page 93)
Scriber or large-pointed needle
Piping bags (cones)
Paintbrushes
Non-stick teflon-coated cloth or greaseproof (parchment) paper
Nos.1 and 0 piping tubes (tips)

1 Marzipan (almond ice) the cake then cover with sugarpaste (rolled fondant) (see pages 12–13). Cover the board with sugarpaste. Leave both to dry. Place the cake on the board.

2 Trace the girl template and scribe it onto the cake. Pipe royal icing (see

Flood in the royal icing into the outline then, with a paintbrush, ease to the corners.

pages 14–15) around the outlines in the appropriate colour, then flood with thinned royal icing. To do this, fill a piping bag (cone) with icing (see pages 14–15) and cut a tiny hole at the end. Pipe the icing into the outline and, with a paintbrush, ease it closer to the outline. Start with the white sections or there is a risk of the red colour bleeding into the white. When you have finished those, flood the areas that appear to be the furthest away, then finish with the areas that appear closest.

3 To make the side pieces, trace the template and place them under a transparent teflon-coated mat or greaseproof (parchment) paper and pipe the outline first. Then, fill in the same way as the girl. Allow at least 24 hours

Pipe the side decorations onto greaseproof paper, leave to dry then gently peel off.

for the designs to dry, then release them and attach to the cake with royal icing.

4 Flood the parcels on the stocking separately and attach them with royal icing when dry. Using a no.1 tube (tip), overpipe the toe and heel areas of the stocking, and add buttons to the front of the gown. Add stiff white royal icing to the edges of the hat and gown. Paint the details of the hair and face outline with skintone food colouring.

5 Trace the greeting template and scribe it onto the cake. Pipe the greeting using a no.1 tube and red royal icing. Attach the ribbon to the base of the cake with royal icing. Attach the three holly leaves on top of the stocking, securing with royal icing.

The coming of the kings

The coming of the kings is celebrated on the 6th of January in many countries. This cake is hand-painted. Do not be afraid to paint directly on the cake – just let the sugarpaste (rolled fondant) dry first then, if you make a mistake, remove it with a dampened sponge.

Cake and decoration

23cm (9in) long, octagonal fruit cake, 15cm (5¾in) deep (see pages 8–9)
750g (1½lb) marzipan (almond icing)
750g (1½lb) ivory sugarpaste (rolled fondant)
30cm (12in) long, octagonal cake board
Chestnut brown, claret, baby blue, mint green, tangerine, melon and black food colourings
Clear alcohol
125g (4oz) white sugarpaste (rolled fondant)

Equipment

Templates (see page 95)
Scriber or large-pointed needle
Paintbrushes
Sponge (optional)
Craft knife

Colour the three kings using claret, baby blue, mint green and tangerine.

1 Marzipan (almond ice) the cake then cover with ivory sugarpaste (rolled fondant) (see pages 12–13). Place the cake on the board.

2 Trace the three kings template and scribe the design on top of the cake.

3 Mix the food colourings with clear alcohol – alcohol will evaporate and dry more quickly than water. All liquids will eat into sugarpaste, so make sure you remove any excess moisture at all times.

4 Start by painting the hills, sand and camels using different strengths of chestnut brown. Proceed onto colouring the three kings with the claret, baby blue, mint green and tangerine food colourings. Paint the star in melon.

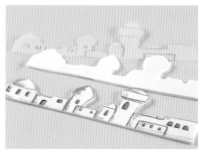

Paint in small windows and doors chestnut brown, shaded with a little black.

Make a wash of very pale baby blue for the sky and down the sides of the cake. You may find it easier to use a sponge for the large areas. Finally, paint in the small buildings in the distance with a little white, outlined with black and chestnut brown.

5 Roll out the white sugarpaste thinly. Trace the template of the buildings to go around the base of the cake and transfer the pattern onto the paste using a scriber. Use the craft knife to cut out the buildings and place them around the sides of the cake. Join the buildings together so there are no gaps and make sure you have a clean edge at the bottom. Paint in small windows and doors using the chestnut brown, shaded with a little black.

Christmas star

This stunning creation combines the beauty of delicate piping and that of the Christmas roses. If you are an experienced sugarcrafter, you may wish to make the roses and mistletoe yourself. Thanks to the mistletoe, this cake will also suit any New Year's table.

Cake and decoration

15cm (6in) star-shaped cake, cut from a round cake of your choice (see pages 8–11)
1kg (2lb) marzipan (almond icing)
25cm (10in) round cake board
1kg (2lb) royal icing
Selection of food colourings
6 bunches of silk or sugar mistletoe
3 silk or sugar Christmas roses with leaves (see page 72)
Decorative ribbon

Equipment

Steel ruler
Side scraper
Piping bags (cones)
Nos.00, 0, 1 and 1.5 piping tubes (tips)
Template (see page 94) and craft knife
Sheet of cardboard
Scriber or large-pointed needle
Posy pick
Double-sided tape

1 Marzipan (almond ice) the cake (see page 12) then place on the round board. Coat the cake with white royal icing (see pages 14–15), starting with the top. Smooth level with the steel ruler. Leave to dry, then ice six alternate sides using the side scraper. When dry, ice the six remaining sides. Repeat this process three to five times until you obtain a smooth finish.

2 When the cake is dry, pipe a thin line around the edge of the board using a no.1.5 piping tube (tip). Thin the icing with water and coat the board. Leave to dry then, with the same tube, pipe a snail trail around the base of the cake.

3 Cut a cardboard template for the side of the cake. Using a scriber, mark the pattern on the cake. Pipe the extension bridge along the curved edges of the design with a no.1 tube, building it to about five lines deep. Leave the piping work to dry thoroughly.

4 When dry, soften a small amount of royal icing with water and paint over the

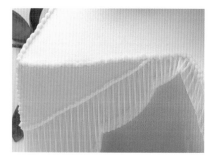

Pipe the extension bridge with a no.1 tube, building it to about five lines deep.

Arrange the Christmas roses and foliage in a posy pick in the centre of the cake.

inside of the extension bridge in order to neaten and strengthen it.

5 Pipe extension lines from the straight edge of the design to the outside of the extension bridge using a no.00 piping tube. Pipe a line of small dots along the straight edge using a no.0 tube. If you wish, continue piping dots around the edges of the cake to obtain a neat finish.

6 Arrange small bunches of mistletoe on the board between the points of the star. Secure with royal icing. Then, arrange the Christmas roses and foliage in a posy pick in the centre of the cake. Attach the ribbon of your choice to the board using double-sided tape. Novice decorators may prefer to omit the piping; the cake will still look very attractive.

Blanket of snow

This miniature Christmas cake is very easy to make and will suit sugarcraft beginners. The design is simple and the combination of white and pale turquoise provides a modern and contemporary feel to the cake. These individual cakes make ideal presents.

Cake and decoration

10cm (4in) square cake of your choice (see pages 8–11)
500g (1lb) marzipan (almond icing)
500g (1lb) pale turquoise sugarpaste (rolled fondant)
15cm (6in) thin, square gold or silver cake board
250g (8oz) white sugarpaste (rolled fondant)
Clear alcohol
30g (1oz) white flowerpaste (gum paste)

Equipment

Sharp knife
Star cutter
Small and large Christmas tree cutters

1 Marzipan (almond ice) the cake then cover with the pale turquoise sugarpaste (rolled fondant) (see pages 12–13). Place the cake on the board and leave to dry thoroughly.

2 Roll out the white sugarpaste to a 3mm (⅛in) thickness. Make sure that the piece is at least 20cm (8in) wide and 15cm (6in) deep. With a sharp knife, cut a random wavy line along the top edge.

3 Brush one half of the cake with clear alcohol, dividing the cake diagonally. Place the piece of white sugarpaste across the cake from corner to corner and smooth down the sides. Trim away the excess paste from the base and corners with the sharp knife.

4 Make a narrow roll from the remaining sugarpaste. Attach it to the base of the cake around the two uncovered sides and smooth the ends into the paste on the corners.

5 Mix together the flowerpaste (gum paste) (see page 15) with an equal amount of sugarpaste and roll out thinly. Using the respective cutters, cut out a star, one large tree and two small trees. Attach the star to the top corner of the cake. Place the trees along the edge of the snow line and trim away at the bases to fit against the curve if necessary.

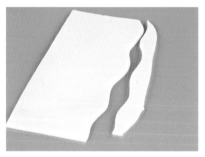

Cut a random wavy line along the top edge of the piece of white sugarpaste.

Place the piece of white sugarpaste across the cake from corner to corner.

Reindeers' night out

All the presents are now delivered, and it is time for the reindeers to let their antlers down! Once you master the modelling techniques, you will enjoy creating lifelike and amusing figures, much to the pleasure of children.

Cake and decoration

30cm (12in) oval fruit cake
(see pages 8–9)
1.25kg (2½lb) marzipan (almond icing)
38cm (15in) oval cake board
1.25kg (2½lb) white sugarpaste
(rolled fondant)
250g (8oz) pastillage
Small quantity of royal icing
Melon, Christmas red, black, green and dark brown food colourings
150g (5oz) poppy red sugarpaste
(rolled fondant)
15g (½oz) black sugarpaste
(rolled fondant)
60g (2oz) peach sugarpaste
(rolled fondant)
500g (1lb) teddy bear brown sugarpaste
(rolled fondant)
Small quantity of brown flowerpaste
(gum paste)
Pale blue dusting powder (petal dust)
Red ribbon

Equipment

Templates (see page 95)
Craft knife
Paintbrushes
Piping bags (cones)
No.1.5 piping tube (tip)
Dresden tool
Small eyelet cutter

1 Marzipan (almond ice) the cake, place it on the board, then cover both with white sugarpaste (rolled fondant) (see pages 12–13).

2 Trace the sleigh templates. Roll out the pastillage (see page 15) and cut out the pieces. Paint a melon border, red centre and black edge. Join the pieces with royal icing (see pages 14–15).

3 To make Santa, see page 82, step 4, but leave him standing. Make the feet bigger to support the body.

4 To make the reindeers, roll 30g (1oz) of brown sugarpaste into a ball for the head. Form a snout and mark the mouth. Glue two small cones of paste to the head for ears, then press down with

a dresden tool. Make five brown noses and a red one for Rudolph. Cut out the eyes using an eyelet cutter and position.

5 Roll a little brown flowerpaste (gum paste) (see page 15) into a long sausage shape. Curve to form antlers. Roll 60g (2oz) of brown sugarpaste for the body and make in the same way as Santa's. Use a craft knife to texture the body, leaving the lower legs smooth. Mark the hooves. Attach the head with icing.

6 Place the reindeers into the sledge. Secure the antlers with icing. Paint the eyes and hooves black. Make beer cans, wine bottles and a small sign and put in place. Pipe icy glaciers around the cake. Shade with light blue and attach the ribbon around the board.

Cut out the sleigh shape from rolled out pastillage and leave to dry flat.

Assemble the reindeers, securing the pieces with a little royal icing.

Santa's sack

This original creation is extremely easy to make and is a favourite with children. Use real sweets or make your own with coloured sugarpaste (rolled fondant) – just make sure there are enough for everyone!

Cake and decoration

20cm (8in) round fruit cake
1kg (2lb) marzipan (almond icing)
1kg (2lb) white sugarpaste
(rolled fondant)
Yellow food colouring
Icing (confectioners') sugar
Clear alcohol
23cm (9in) round, silver or gold
cake board
Decorative cord or ribbon
Decorations, wrapped sweets
and chocolates

Equipment

Paintbrush

1 Marzipan (almond ice) the cake (see page 12) and leave on a spare board to dry thoroughly.

2 Lightly tint the white sugarpaste (rolled fondant) (see page 13) with yellow food colouring and roll into a circle on a surface that has been dusted with icing (confectioners') sugar. The circle of yellow paste should be at least 5mm (¼in) thick, so it does not tear. Also make sure that it is large enough to cover the side of the cake and form the folds of the sack when brought together on top of the cake.

3 Using a clean paintbrush, brush the marzipan all over with clear alcohol and place the cake in the centre of the circle of yellow paste. Gather the sugarpaste

up the side of the cake and pleat to form the neck, leaving an opening to place the decorations in. If necessary, press the sugarpaste onto the alcohol to secure in place. Leave the paste to dry thoroughly then transfer the cake to the cake board.

4 Tie a decorative cord or ribbon loosely around the neck. Dust with sifted icing sugar and fill the opening with the decorations, wrapped sweets and chocolates of your choice.

Tip: If preferred, make your own decorative ribbon with red and green strips of sugarpaste entwined together.

Fill the top of the cake with a selection of Christmas decorations and sweets.

Tie the cord loosely around the neck of the sack with the ends draping down the side.

Merry Christmas cake

This exquisite Christmas cake is quite versatile. You can add any festive figures made of modelling paste if you wish. You can also personalize the greeting or colour it green to match the Christmas trees.

Cake and decoration

23cm (9in) round fruit cake
(see pages 8–9)
1kg (2lb) marzipan (almond icing)
1kg (2lb) white sugarpaste
(rolled fondant)
25cm (10in) round cake board
Green, yellow, red plus a selection of food colourings
Small quantity of royal icing
Icing (confectioners') sugar
1 egg white
Decorative ribbon

Equipment

Scissors
Star cutters
Paintbrush
Piping bags (cones)
Holly cutters

With a pair of scissors, shape the trees from cones of green sugarpaste.

1 Marzipan (almond ice) the cake then cover with white sugarpaste (rolled fondant) (see pages 12–13). Leave to dry then place onto the cake board.

2 To make the Christmas trees, colour some sugarpaste green and roll into cone shapes. Use scissors to make snips into the side of the cone all over. Leave to dry. Then, colour some paste yellow, roll out and, using the cutters, cut out small stars. Leave to dry, then secure the stars on the top of the tree with a little royal icing (see pages 14–15). Dust with sifted icing (confectioners') sugar.

3 To make the presents, mould some sugarpaste in various sizes and shapes. Leave to dry. Paint in different colours and leave to dry. Then, paint on bows and ribbons, stripes and spots. Arrange on the cake, securing with royal icing.

4 Draw the greeting onto a piece of tracing paper in simple, easy-to-read letters (trace them from a lettering book or greeting card if you wish). Place the paper on a spare board and cover with greaseproof (parchment) paper. Colour some royal icing red and spoon into a piping bag (cone). Pipe around the outline of the letters first, then fill in the centre. If the icing is too stiff and fails to sit flat, brush it with a paintbrush dipped in egg white. Leave to dry overnight, then peel the letters and position them on the cake, securing with a little royal icing.

5 To make the holly leaves, roll out some sugarpaste and, using the cutters, cut out holly shapes. Shape the leaves to add movement and leave to dry. When dry, paint them green. Then, roll small amounts of paste into tiny balls to make the holly berries. Paint them red and leave to dry thoroughly. Position them onto the cake. Finally, attach the ribbon around the cake with a little icing.

Tip: Never use real holly berries to decorate your cake – they are toxic!

Paint small pieces of sugarpaste different colours to make the presents.

The carol singer

Christmas carols are an essential element to the Christmas festivities. In this project, the design is hand-painted on a plaque and then placed on the cake. Remove the plaque as a keepsake before the cake is eaten.

Cake and decoration

250g (8oz) pastillage
20cm (8in) round fruit cake
(see pages 8–9)
750g (1½lb) marzipan (almond icing)
750g (1½lb) white sugarpaste
(rolled fondant)
Christmas red, chestnut brown, spruce green, white, baby blue and primrose food colourings
Clear alcohol
Small quantity of royal icing
Small quantity of flowerpaste
(gum paste)
Decorative red ribbon

Equipment

12.5cm (5in) round plaque cutter
Closed curve crimpers
Template (see page 95)
Scriber or large-pointed needle
Craft knife
Paintbrushes
Lace cutter (J)
Large Christmas rose and ivy leaf cutters
Rose veiner
Ball tool
Piping bags (cones) and tubes (tips)
26g green wire and florists' tape

1 Roll out the pastillage (see page 15) and, with the cutter, cut out a plaque.

Marzipan (almond ice) the cake, then cover the cake and board with sugarpaste (rolled fondant) (see pages 12–13). Crimp the edge of the board.

2 Trace the template and scribe it onto the dry plaque. Place the plaque in the centre of the cake, and cut around it. Remove the sugarpaste, leaving the marzipan. Put the plaque in place to ensure that it fits, then remove.

3 Use red to paint the door and chestnut brown to outline the features of the boy, girl and cat. Paint the ivy leaves and Christmas tree spruce green. Paint the snow white and the girl's dress baby blue. Mix the food colourings with clear alcohol so they dry more quickly.

4 Secure the dry plaque in position with royal icing (see pages 14–15). Cut out several lace pieces from flowerpaste (gum paste) (see page 15). These will hide the join between the cake and the plaque. Secure with royal icing.

5 To make the Christmas roses, cut out five petals in white flowerpaste. Vein the petals and ball the outer edges. Join the base of the petals together to form the centre of the rose and leave

Paint the scene using food colourings and leave to dry thoroughly.

to dry. Colour some royal icing primrose and pipe small dots in the centre of the flower (see page 28). Make six roses.

6 To make the ivy leaves, colour a small amount of flowerpaste spruce green. Roll out the paste on a grooved board. Cut out 12 large ivy leaves. Ball the outer edge of the leaf, then push a moistened green wire into the groove at the back of the leaf. Leave to dry then, using spruce green, paint darker areas in the centre part of the leaf. Tape two leaves together, leaving a gap to place a Christmas rose in the middle.

7 Position the roses and leaves around the cake and secure with a little royal icing. Finally, attach the red ribbon around the board.

Christmas sleigh

A side flange is used on this cake to emphasize the attractive shape of the scalloped oval cake, with its elegant run-out sleigh and frosty icicles and snowballs. The decorative details on this cake are superb to look at.

Cake and decoration

20 x 15cm (8 x 6in) scalloped, oval cake of your choice (see pages 8–9)
750g (1½lb) marzipan (almond icing)
30 x 25cm (12 x 10in) scalloped, oval cake board
750g (1½lb) royal icing
Caster (superfine) sugar
Green and red food colourings
Decorative ribbon

Equipment

Scriber and template (see page 92)
Piping bags (cones)
No.1, 2 and 3 piping tubes (tips)
Shaped side scraper

1 Marzipan (almond ice) the cake (see page 12), then coat cake and board with royal icing (see pages 14–15).

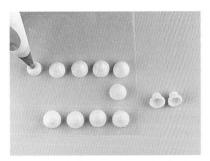

To make the bells, pipe a tapered bulb of icing then, once dry, scoop out the centre.

2 Scribe a line around the centre of the cake. Pipe a line of icing along the line. Take the scraper around the cake to leave the bold flange in place. Allow to dry, then make a base flange the same way. Pipe a bold line at the base of the cake then neaten with a scraper. Dry.

3 Pipe the icicles at the top edge of the cake, using a no.2 piping tube (tip). Dredge caster (superfine) sugar over them, before they begin to crust. When dry, brush excess sugar away.

4 Using a no.3 piping tube, pipe white bulbs at the base border. Pipe similar bulbs at the top border but leave space between each bud for a further bulb to be piped. Dredge all these piped bulbs with caster sugar. Allow to dry, then brush away excess sugar. Pipe extra bulbs between the existing ones.

5 To make the bells, use a no.3 piping tube to pipe a tapered bulb on top of a flat bulb on greaseproof (parchment) paper. Dredge with caster sugar at once. When the outer surface has formed a crust, gently scoop out the soft centre with a cocktail stick (toothpick). Leave to dry, then pipe plain shells around the base of the flange using a no.2 tube.

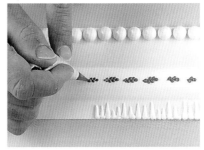

Using a no.1 tube, pipe small holly leaves with green icing and tiny berries with red.

6 Trace the sleigh template and scribe it onto the cake. Pipe the linework using a no.1 tube, first in white icing and then overpipe in green. Fill in with red icing and decorate with white. When dry, position the run-out pieces on the cake, securing with a little royal icing. If you prefer, you can replace the sleigh design with a bought Christmas ornament.

7 Pipe a line inside the top border on the cake using a no.3 tube. Attach sugar bells at the end of the line. Pipe holly and berries onto the plain bulbs on the top border and around the edge of the board. Secure the ribbon around the flange with royal icing. Fix the sugar bells with icing and pipe holly and berries. Trim the board with ribbon.

Golden tree cake

Instead of white sugarpaste, this creation uses royal icing, beaten to a thick consistency. Royal icing enables you to texture the snow for a more rugged look. For this particular recipe, artificial decorations have been used but feel free to make your own.

Cake and decoration

23cm (9in) square fruit cake
(see pages 8–9)
1kg (2lb) marzipan (almond icing)
500g (1lb) royal icing
Artificial Christmas tree, holly leaves
and berries
Icing (confectioners') sugar
Wide decorative ribbon or two thinner
ones, overlapping
Organza bow

Equipment

Palette knife

1 Marzipan (almond ice) the square fruit cake (see page 12), then cover the top with royal icing (see pages 14–15), forming decorative peaks with a palette knife.

2 Place a plastic tree or similar suitable decoration in one corner with some artificial holly and berries. Then, dust with sifted icing (confectioners') sugar.

3 Tie a wide ribbon around the sides of the cake or overlap two thinner ribbons for a layered effect. Secure the ribbon at the back with a little royal icing. Leave the icing to dry thoroughly.

4 Add a coloured bow, made from organza or similar material, to the front corner.

Place an organza bow on the front corner of the cake.

Tip: If you prefer to make your own decorations, buy specially shaped cutters to cut the Christmas trees and holly leaves and berries from sugarpaste (rolled fondant) (see page 14). Leave them to dry thoroughly before positioning them on the cake.

Dust the decorations and royal icing with sieved icing sugar.

Triple truffle cake

There is a simple rule in life ... you can never have too much chocolate, especially at Christmas time. This recipe features dark, milk and white chocolates, and all play starring roles in this chocaholic's extravaganza.

Cake and decoration

23cm (9in) round chocolate mud cake (see page 10)
250g (8oz) dark chocolate, chopped
125ml (4floz/½cup) cream
165g (5½oz/⅔cup) sugar
300g (10oz) Madeira cake crumbs
2tbsp jam (jelly) of your choice
3tbsp cream
60g (2oz/¼cup) unsalted butter, melted
300g (10oz) milk or dark chocolate, melted
2tbsp rum
150g (5oz) each of white, milk and dark chocolate
Egg white
24 carat edible gold leaf

Equipment

Paintbrush
Tweezers

1 Cut the dome off the cake to give a flat surface. Turn the cake upside down on a rack over a tray to catch the glaze.

2 To make the glaze, put 250ml (8oz) of dark chocolate in a pan with the cream and sugar and stir continuously over a low heat until smooth. Bring to the boil, then reduce the heat and simmer for 5 minutes, stirring

occasionally to keep it from sticking. Remove from the heat and stir gently.

3 Pour the glaze over the cake, letting it run evenly down the side. Tap the tray on your working area to level the surface. Leave to set completely.

4 To make the truffles, line a tray with greaseproof (parchment) paper. Mix the cake crumbs, jam (jelly), cream, butter and rum with 300g (10oz) of melted milk or dark chocolate. Refrigerate for 20 to 30 minutes or until firm. Roll teaspoons of the mixture into balls and place on the tray. Refrigerate for 10 to 15 minutes or until firm.

5 Line three trays with greaseproof paper. Melt the remaining white, milk

and dark chocolates separately: put the chocolate in a heatproof bowl, bring a pan of water to a simmer, remove from the heat and place over the pan, making sure the bowl does not touch the water. Stir the chocolate until melted.

6 Using a fork, dip the truffles in the chocolates, tapping on the edge of the bowl to drain any excess. Dip a third of the truffles in the white chocolate, a third in the milk and the rest in the dark. Leave on the trays to set.

7 Dab a spot of egg white onto the dark chocolate truffles, then remove the gold leaf from the sheet with tweezers and press onto the egg white. Put the cake on a serving plate and pile the truffles on top.

Use a fork, or a special chocolate dipper, to cover the truffles with chocolate.

Remove the gold leaf from the sheet with tweezers and press onto the truffles.

Starry night

This cake is easier to make than it looks. The combination of raspberries and chocolate is a well-known perfect match. The white chocolate and mascarpone mousse is pure indulgence and adds a light contrast to the rich mud cake.

Cake and decoration

23cm (9in) round chocolate mud cake (see page 10)
300g (10oz/2cups) fresh raspberries, or frozen raspberries, thawed and drained
2 eggs
60g (2oz/¼cup) sugar
200g (7oz) white chocolate, melted and cooled
250g (8oz/1cup) mascarpone cheese
2tbsp Grand Marnier
2tbsp orange juice
2tsp gelatine
250ml (8floz/1cup) cream, whipped
Cocoa powder
150g (5oz) dark chocolate drops
Decorative ribbon (optional)

Equipment

Electric mixer
Flat-bladed knife
Sheet of cardboard and craft knife

1 Invert the cake onto a flat serving plate. Put the cleaned ring part of the tin (pan) you used to bake the cake in back around the cake – not the base. Sprinkle the raspberries over the top, leaving a 1cm (½in) gap around the edge.

2 To make the top layer, beat the eggs and sugar until thick and increased

Cover the raspberries with the white chocolate mousse mixture.

in volume. On low speed, beat in the chocolate, mascarpone and Grand Marnier until combined, making sure not to overbeat. Place the orange juice in a bowl and sprinkle on the gelatine in an even layer. Leave until the gelatine is spongy – do not stir. Bring a small pan of water to the boil, remove from the heat and place the bowl in the pan. The water should come halfway up the sides of the bowl. Stir the gelatine until clear and dissolved. Allow to cool slightly. Stir into the chocolate mixture, then gently fold in the whipped cream.

3 Spoon the mousse onto the cooled cake base, covering the raspberries and making sure it reaches the side of the tin. Smooth the surface. Refrigerate for 2 hours, or until set.

4 Run a flat-bladed knife around the inside of the tin. Cut a large star shape from a piece of cardboard and use as a stencil over the cake, resting the cardboard over the tin and dusting generously with cocoa powder, to make a large chocolate star on the top. Carefully remove the tin.

5 Cut a piece of greaseproof (parchment) paper as wide as the tin is high, and long enough to fit around the cake. Melt the chocolate drops, cool slightly and spread over the paper, right up to the edges. Wrap the paper around the cake, chocolate side against the cake, before the chocolate sets. Leave for the chocolate to set, then gently peel away the paper. Attach a ribbon if desired.

Make a star on the top of the cake using cocoa powder and a cardboard stencil.

Santa and the penguins

If you prefer to make a fun cake rather than a more traditional one, then this is the perfect cake for you. The amusing scene will delight your guests and make you most popular with the children, who will probably want to play with the skiing penguins!

Cake and decoration

30cm (12in) long octagonal fruit cake, 19cm (7½in) deep (see pages 8–9)
1.5kg (3lb) marzipan (almond icing)
36 x 25cm (14 x 10in) octagonal cake board
1.75kg (3½lb) white sugarpaste (rolled fondant)
18cm (7in) round fruit cake
20cm (8in) thin, square board
Granulated sugar
150g (5oz) black sugarpaste (rolled fondant)
Small quantity of royal icing
Black and melon paste food colourings
Spaghetti
185g (6oz) poppy red sugarpaste (rolled fondant)
60g (2oz) each of peach and chocolate brown sugarpastes (rolled fondant)
Decorative ribbon

Equipment

Piping bag (cone)
Piping tube (tip)
Eyelet cutter
Selection of modelling tools

1 Marzipan (almond ice) the octagonal cake, then cover the cake and board with white sugarpaste (rolled fondant) (see pages 12–13).

For the penguins, use ready-coloured sugarpastes rather than food colourings.

2 Cut the round cake into mountain shapes then place onto the thin board. Marzipan, then cover with sugarpaste. Place on the octagonal cake. Sprinkle the mountain tops with sugar.

3 To make the penguins, roll 7g (¼oz) of black paste into a cone. Shape the head. Cut two small V shapes in the body for wings. Indent holes for the eyes and beak, then pipe in with icing. When dry, paint the eyes black and the beak melon. Colour some paste melon and form feet. Make a white oval for the front of the body. Secure all elements with water. To make the ski poles, use spaghetti and flatten melon paste onto the end. Push into the body. Make strips of red paste and shape into skis. Place on the cake, securing with icing.

4 To make Santa, roll 125g (4oz) of red paste. Pull out two arms and two legs. Bend to a sitting position. Use peach paste to form the hands. Secure to the arms with icing. Roll 22g (¾oz) of peach paste for the head. Indent a mouth, then make the nose and cheeks. Cut out two eyes, then paint black. Secure with water. Make a red hat and black shoes. Secure all elements to the body with icing. Cut white strips for the fur. Make a black belt and yellow buckle. Secure with water. Pipe icing for his beard and hair and add a bobble to his hat.

5 To make the sack, roll 60g (2oz) of brown paste into a ball. Hollow then pull to mould the top. Make presents and position, securing with icing. Attach the ribbon around the board.

Assemble the Santa on a flat surface before placing onto the cake.

Candlelight

This creation is a traditional royal-iced cake, which is simply but attractively decorated with run-out candles and cut-out holly leaves. The simplicity of the design conveys an elegant feel to the cake.

Cake and decoration

20 x 15cm (8 x 6in) oval fruit cake
(see pages 8–9)
1kg (2lb) marzipan (almond icing)
30 x 25cm (12 x 10in) oval
cake board
1kg (2lb) sugarpaste (rolled fondant)
Small quantity of royal icing
Melon, black, tangerine, dark cream and
Christmas green paste food colourings
60g (2oz) flowerpaste (gum paste)
Strong red powder food colouring
Narrow and wide peach ribbon

Equipment

Template (see page 94) and scriber
Glass or Perspex and double-sided tape
Nos.1 and 2 piping tubes (tips)
Piping bags (cones)
Paintbrush
Cranked palette knife
Craft knife

1 Marzipan (almond ice) the cake, then cover the cake and board with sugarpaste (rolled fondant) (see pages 12–13). Leave to dry, then attach the cake to the board with royal icing (see pages 14–15).

2 Trace the candles and circle from the template and attach it to the glass

Pipe around the motifs in melon royal icing, then fill in with the appropriate icings.

with tape. Cover with greaseproof (parchment) paper and secure with tape. Using the no.1 piping tube (tip), outline the design with royal icing. Set aside enough icing to outline 'Noel' and pipe a snail trail. Thin the rest with water and colour three-quarters with melon. Flood the circle around the candles. Leave each area to dry as you work.

3 Flood the candles with white icing, then pipe melted wax with the no.2 tube. Colour a little icing black and pipe the wicks with the no.1 tube. Colour a little icing tangerine and pipe the flame with the no.1 tube. Paint on the darker inner flame. Remove from the paper with the palette knife and attach to the cake with icing. Pipe dots of icing around the circle with the no.1 tube.

Remove the circle from the greaseproof paper and attach to the cake with icing.

4 Trace the leaves and twigs from the template and scribe them onto the cake. Colour some icing cream and pipe the twigs with the no.1 tube. Colour the flowerpaste (gum paste) (see page 15) green and cut out the holly leaves, using the template as a guide. Twist the leaves and secure to the cake with icing. Colour some icing red and pipe the berries using the no.2 tube. Paint a dark spot on each berry and paint the veins of the leaves with dark green.

5 Pipe around 'Noel' with the reserved icing and the no.1 tube, then flood in. Leave to dry then pipe a snail trail around the base of the cake with the no.1 tube. Attach two thin peach ribbons above the trail and the thicker one around the cake board.

Silver cake

This stunning cake is a perfect example of how a simple cake can look truly beautiful. The silver dragées add a sparkling festive effect, and the shiny silver ribbon delicately finishes off the cake.

Cake and decoration

23cm (9in) fruit cake (see pages 8–9)
1kg (2lb) marzipan (almond icing)
1kg (2lb) sugarpaste (rolled fondant)
25cm (10in) square silver cake board
Icing (confectioners') sugar
Egg white
Decorative silver ribbon
Small quantity of royal icing
Silver dragées in assorted sizes

Equipment

Paintbrush
Small piping bag (cone)
Tweezers

1 Marzipan (almond ice) the cake then cover with white sugarpaste (rolled fondant) (see pages 12–13), reserving a small amount of sugarpaste for decoration. Once thoroughly dry, place the cake onto the square silver board.

2 On a surface lightly dusted with icing (confectioners') sugar, roll out the reserved sugarpaste into several long, thin strips. Twist two of the strips together to form a rope. With a paintbrush, brush a little egg white around the bottom edge of the cake and wrap the rope around the cake, hiding any joins you may need to make (try to make these joins at the back of the cake so they do not show). Set aside for a few hours, or leave overnight, to dry thoroughly.

Tie a big bow on top of the cake so that it looks like a wrapped Christmas gift.

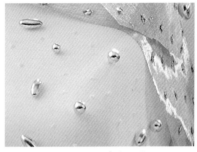

Use tweezers to position silver dragées randomly over the cake.

3 Cut a length of ribbon long enough to run from the base on one side of the cake to the base on the other, and gently tuck it under the rope. Cut two more lengths of ribbon long enough to tuck under the rope edge and be tied together into a big bow.

4 Fill a small piping bag (cone) with white royal icing (see pages 14–15) and pipe dots randomly all over the cake. Using tweezers, secure assorted sized silver dragées onto the icing dots and leave to dry thoroughly.

Sparkling stars

This miniature cake is simple yet modern. It makes a stylish change from the traditional green and red colour scheme. Why not make one for every guest to finish the meal in style, or as a gift to take home?

Cake and decoration

10cm (4in) square fruit cake
(see pages 8–9)
250g (8oz) marzipan (almond icing)
250g (8oz) light blue sugarpaste
(rolled fondant)
15cm (6in) thin, square gold or
silver cake board
60g (2oz) white sugarpaste
(rolled fondant)
60g (2oz) white flowerpaste (gum paste)
Edible glue
Granulated sugar
Small quantity of royal icing

Equipment

Templates (see page 92)
Craft knife
Small star cutter
Piping bag (cone)
No.1 piping tube (tip)

1 Marzipan (almond ice) the cake then cover with the light blue sugarpaste (rolled fondant) (see pages 12–13). Leave the cake to dry thoroughly then place on the board.

2 Mix together the white sugarpaste and flowerpaste (gum paste) (see page 15) and roll out thinly. Trace the two star templates and cut out one of each from the paste. Use the cutter to cut out a small star. Leave them to dry.

3 From the same paste, cut out 12 triangles, using the template provided. Leave to dry thoroughly, then brush the surface of the stars and triangles with edible glue and sprinkle liberally with granulated sugar. Shake off the excess and leave to dry.

Brush the surface of the stars with edible glue then sprinkle with granulated sugar.

Secure a circle of paste on the top centre of the cake, then position the largest star.

4 Attach two triangles at each corner with a little royal icing (see pages 14–15). Place a triangle in the centre of each side and fill in the gaps with piped bulbs of icing, using a no.1 piping tube (tip).

5 Roll out the remaining paste to a 5mm (¼in) thickness and cut out a 2.5cm (1in) circle shape. Position on the top centre of the cake, securing with a little royal icing. Lay the largest star on top of the circle of paste, lining the points up with the corners of the cake. Then, attach the medium star, laying it on top of the large one and alternating the points. Stand the smallest star on top upright in the centre of the cake. This design could be copied onto a larger cake if desired.

Gingerbread house

Often associated with the characters Hansel and Gretel, this gingerbread house makes a good cake alternative for a Christmas party. Before positioning the roof, fill the house with chocolate and sweet treats for an extra surprise.

Cake and decoration

Dark gingerbread mixture
(see pages 10–11)
200g (7oz) royal icing
28 x 20cm (11 x 18in) cake board
10 small ratafia biscuits (cookies)
15 to 18 chocolates or small truffles
90g (3oz/½cup) chocolate-covered raisins
Small packet candy-covered chocolates
7 small wafer-thin chocolate biscuits (cookies)
1 small chocolate-covered fudge bar, thinly sliced

Equipment

Templates (see page 93) and craft knife
4cm (1½in) round cutter
Palette knife

1 Preheat the oven to 200ºC/ 400ºF/ gas mark 6 and grease two baking (cookie) sheets. Trace the templates for the house and cut out. Thinly roll out the gingerbread dough and cut out the shapes. Cut out the door, then trim 5mm (¼in) off the base of the door. Cut out a window above the door using the round cutter.

2 Transfer the shapes to the baking (cookie) sheets, including the door, and bake for 15 minutes until slightly risen. Leave on the sheets for 2 minutes, then transfer to a wire cooling rack.

3 Spread a little royal icing (see pages 14–15) along the base and up the sides of one side section. Spread more icing along the base of the front section and secure the two sections together on the board, propping them up with small glasses or tumblers for support. Secure the back section, then the other side, and leave for about 30 minutes to set.

4 Spread more icing over the top edges of the side pieces and secure one of the roof sections, again using glasses or tumblers for support. Spread a little icing along the top of the roof and secure the other piece in place.

5 Using a palette knife, spread a thin layer of icing over the roof. For the icicles, hold a teaspoon of icing at an angle above the edges of the roof. As the icing starts to slip from the spoon, catch it along the edges, to create the impression of dancing icicles.

6 Place the ratafia biscuits (cookies), chocolates and chocolate-covered raisins on the roof. Add a single row

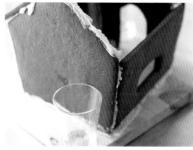

Secure the side sections of the house using a glass or tumbler for support.

of chocolate raisins along the top of the roof for the top tiles. Ice the board.

7 Pipe a little icing onto the backs of the candy-covered chocolates and position them on the house to decorate. Finally, pipe along the edges around the door and along the corners of the cottage.

Position the ratafia biscuits, chocolates and chocolate-covered raisins on the roof.

Templates

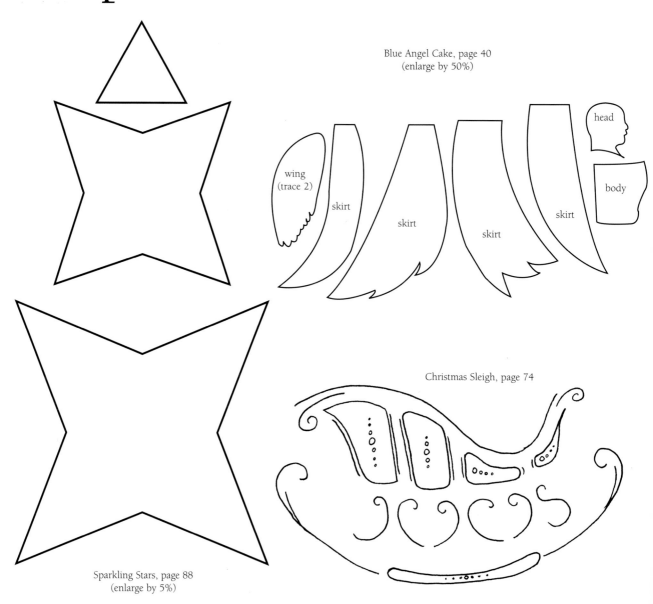

Blue Angel Cake, page 40
(enlarge by 50%)

wing
(trace 2)

skirt

skirt

skirt

skirt

head

body

Sparkling Stars, page 88
(enlarge by 5%)

Christmas Sleigh, page 74

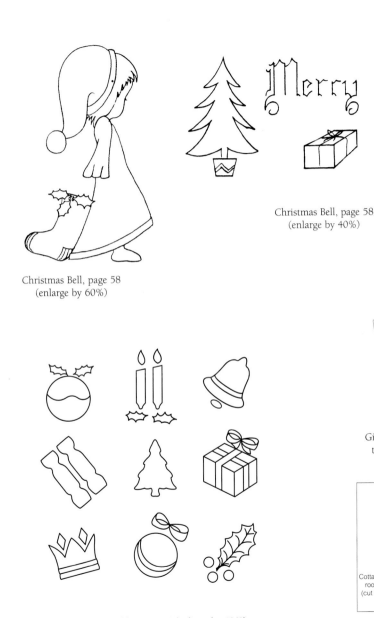

Christmas Bell, page 58
(enlarge by 40%)

Christmas Bell, page 58
(enlarge by 60%)

Cottage front and back
(cut one with door shape,
one without)

Gingerbread House, page 90 (enlarge roof
template by 254% and sides by 246%)

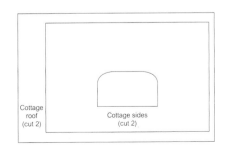

Cottage
roof
(cut 2)

Cottage sides
(cut 2)

Nine-square Sparkle, page 36 (enlarge by 42%)

Christmas Star, page 62
(enlarge by 29%)

Noel

Candlelight, page 84
(enlarge by 160%)

wing
(cut 2)

tail

The Last Christmas Post, page 46
(enlarge by 20%)

Winter Wonderland, page 50
(enlarge by 45%)

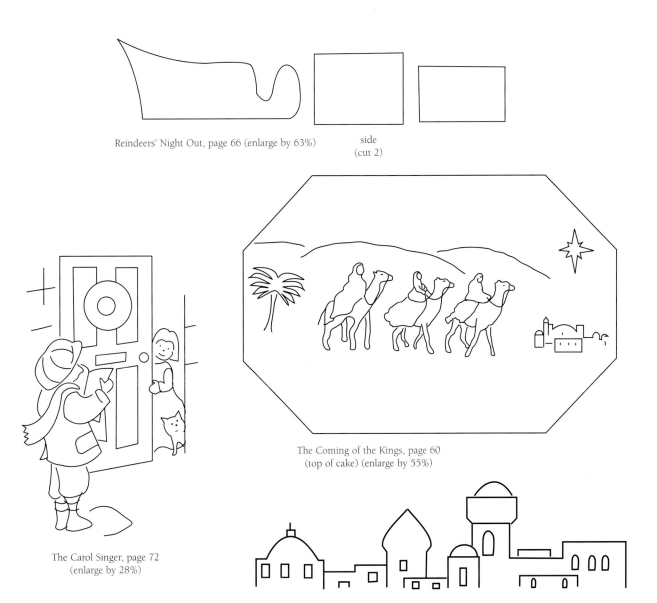

Reindeers' Night Out, page 66 (enlarge by 63%)

side
(cut 2)

The Coming of the Kings, page 60
(top of cake) (enlarge by 55%)

The Carol Singer, page 72
(enlarge by 28%)

The Coming of the Kings, page 60
(sides of cake) (enlarge by 27%)

First published in 2001 by Murdoch Books UK Ltd
Merehurst is an imprint of Murdoch Books UK Ltd
Copyright © 2001 Murdoch Books UK Ltd

ISBN 1 85391 820 2

Project Editor: Carine Tracanelli
Designer: Shahid Mahmood
Photographers: Craig Cranko, James Duncan, Laurence Hudghton, Chris Jones, Reg Morrison,
Zul Mukhida, Ian O'Leary, Craig Robertson, Clive Streeter and Graham Tann
Stylists: Alison Adams, Cath Garrick, May Harris, Mel Housden, Penny Markham and Kerry Mullins.

CEO: Juliet Rogers
Publisher: Kay Scarlett
•

Murdoch Books UK Ltd
Erico House, 6th Floor North,
93-99 Upper Richmond Rd, Putney,
London SW15 2TG
Phone: + 44 (0) 20 8355 1480
Fax: + 44 (0) 20 8355 1499
Murdoch Books UK Ltd is a subsidiary
of Murdoch Magazines Pty Ltd.

Colour separation by Colourscan, Singapore
Printed through Phoenix Offset in China

Murdoch Books®
Pier 8/9, 23 Hickson Road
Millers Point, NSW 2000, Australia
Tel: +61 (0)2 8220 2000
Fax: +61 (0)2 8220 2558
Murdoch Books® is a division
of Murdoch Magazines Pty Ltd.

Culpitt Cake Art
Culpitt Ltd
Jubilee Industrial Estate
Ashington
Northumberland NE63 8UQ
Tel: +44 (0)1670 814 545

Edable Art
1 Stanhope Close
The Grange

Spennymoor
County Durham DL16 6LZ
Tel: +44 (0)1388 816 309

Guy, Paul & Co Ltd
Unit B4 Foundry Way
Little End Road
Eaton Socon
Cambs PE19 3JH
Tel: +44 (0)1480 472 545

Holly Products
Holly Cottage, Hassall Green
Sandbach
Cheshire CW11 4YA
Tel: +44 (0)1270 761 403

Renshaw Scott Ltd
Crown Street
Liverpool L8 7RF
Tel: +44 (0)151 706 8200

Sparkling Sugarcraft
361 Bury Old Road
Prestwich M25 1PY
Tel: +44 (0)161 773 3033

Squires Kitchen
Squires House
3 Waverley Lane
Farnham, Surrey GU9 8BB
Tel: +44 (0)1252 711 749